The Science of Reading

DK Learning

The Science of Reading

The brain science, language development and phonemic awareness behind the movement

Contents

Introduction	6
Reading and the Brain	8
Models and Theories of Reading	10
Foundational Reading Skills	20
Advanced Reading Skills and Strategies	54
Text and Genre Study	86
Oral Language Development	96
Assessment and Intervention	118
Instructional Strategies and Equity in Literacy	134
The Alphabetic Code	182
Debunking Reading Myths	184
Jargon Buster	186
Index	190
Bibliography	196
About the Authors and Acknowledgments	202

Introduction

by Tami Reis-Frankfort

Thirty years ago, I stepped into my first teaching job in an inner-city London primary school. Fresh out of teacher training, brimming with ideas, I was determined to enthuse my class and immerse them in the love of reading. With story reading at the end of every day, colourful, enticing book displays of different genres and topics, story writing and book making, and many more creative ideas, I would make sure that my pupils would share my passion for reading and learn to read. And yet, many didn't. I soon realised that I had no tools to teach the children who hadn't figured out how to teach themselves to read. They needed reading instruction, but this wasn't part of my training, and I felt a sense of guilt as I handed over my non-readers to their next teacher. I didn't know how to teach the most important subject a child comes to school to learn – reading!

At the very same time, multiple studies were being published across different disciplines (neuroscience, psychology, special needs

education, linguistics, communication studies – to name a few) and amassing a growing body of knowledge on how the brain learns to read and write and how to prevent reading failure. These studies were confined to the musty corridors of academia, often dismissed and derided by educators and administrators. Reading instruction was considered the realm of a teacher's personal philosophy and there was no place for dogged research to dictate how to teach it. At the same time, too many pupils were failing to learn to read. The lucky ones would be offered extra support in small groups. The very lucky ones had parents who could afford private tuition. Many pupils were not so fortunate. They left school unable to pursue their dreams because they couldn't read.

Happily, the tide has turned. The Science of Reading has broken out of those musty corridors and is now informing educators, administrators, legislators and parents, and even changing the curriculum in teacher preparation courses. Reading instruction is undergoing a transformation. And it is not a fad; it is here to stay. In the age of information, it is no longer possible to ignore research. Teachers are embracing the Science of Reading because they know that when they inform their teaching with research they will succeed, and their pupils will succeed too.

Now more than 40 states across the United States have passed laws to reform reading so that it is more aligned with research. The journey of the Science of Reading has just begun. As with any science, new research that emerges will inform our knowledge and help us hone our understanding and teaching skills.

As we learn more about the Science of Reading and how to align our teaching to the research, we will do better! This book is a great place to start.

Tami Reis-Frankfort
Founder of Phonic Books

"Do the best you can until you know better. Then when you know better, do better."

Maya Angelou

Reading and the Brain

by Dr. Chase Young

As emergent readers understand the alphabetic principle they move into the beginning reading phase. The alphabetic principle is achieved when readers exhibit letter-sound correspondence. Learning to decode print and understand it is necessary for reading.

Early reading stages

When beginning readers access the phonological and orthographic systems to decode print, they utilise the sounds stored in the frontal lobe. These sounds help them decode the print; phonics initiates the reading process, and the first cognitive stop is the frontal lobe. Phonemic awareness, which involves recognising and manipulating individual sounds, is crucial in the early stages of reading. This ability activates the superior temporal gyrus in the brain, which is involved in processing the sounds of speech. Early instruction that builds phonemic awareness supports neural growth and strengthens connections between the frontal and temporal lobes.

However, simply barking at print (a term borrowed from S. J. Samuels) is not reading. Beginning readers must decode and ascribe meaning to the morphemes. When they successfully decode a word, they access the temporal lobe to ascribe meaning.

As beginning readers become more adept at connecting phonemes and grouping them into larger chunks, they engage in the process called blending. After developing their understanding and applying their knowledge of phonemes, using onsets and rimes can aid the process of becoming more automatic. The angular gyrus, which connects the frontal, temporal and occipital lobes, helps integrate phonological,

In the early stages of reading, children use the sounds stored in the frontal lobe to help them decode print.

Readers use numerous mental processes as they learn to decode print.

> "Eventually, beginning readers achieve a level of automaticity that propels them into the next stage of reading."

orthographic and semantic information, facilitating both the decoding of words and the comprehension of their meanings. With practice, readers progress into the fluent decoding stage, where they can rapidly recognise words and ascribe meaning. At the word level, the occipital lobe is engaged, particularly through the visual word form area (VWFA), which is essential for recognising written words and mapping them to their corresponding sounds and meanings. This region becomes more specialised for word recognition as the reader becomes increasingly fluent, which streamlines the reading process.

The next stage of reading

Eventually, beginning readers achieve a level of automaticity that propels them into the next stage of reading. The cerebellum also plays a significant role in this progression by contributing to the fluency and coordination required for automaticity. It aids in fine motor skills, such as tracking text with the eyes, and supports the smooth execution of reading processes as neural pathways become more specialised.

There is a reading pathway located on the left side of the brain, with research identifying specific processes linked to various brain regions. For example, the arcuate fasciculus, a bundle of nerve fibres, plays a critical role in connecting the frontal and temporal lobes, facilitating phonological processing and language comprehension. Additionally, the VWFA in the occipitotemporal region is essential for word recognition. These interconnected systems highlight the complexity and coordination required for reading. The frontal lobe handles short-term memory and phonological processing, while the occipital lobe manages long-term memory, particularly regarding visual word recognition. Studies do not suggest long-term memories are formed before short-term ones, so examining the frontal and temporal lobes is essential to understanding early reading development.

The frontal lobe is responsible for letter-sound correspondence, while the temporal lobe handles semantics. These areas interact with the angular gyrus and the parietal lobe during the reading process, integrating phonological, orthographic and semantic information. The angular gyrus acts as a hub that connects these regions, facilitating higher-order processing necessary for comprehension and the transition from decoding to fluent reading. Linearly, it seems logical that the frontal lobe is the first step in the reading process, followed by the temporal lobe and eventually the occipital lobe. However, linearity may oversimplify this complex process.

Bringing it all together

As readers learn to decode with the frontal lobe, they must simultaneously engage the temporal lobe to ascribe meaning. Over time, the reciprocal relationship between these regions becomes automatic, allowing the occipital lobe to drive the reading process.

Models and Theories of Reading

The Simple View of Reading	12
The Reading Rope	14
Understanding Reading Levels	18

The Simple View of Reading

by Dr. Chase Young

The Simple View of Reading is a foundational framework in literacy education that highlights the interplay between decoding and language comprehension in developing effective reading skills and fostering comprehension.

The Simple View of Reading (SVR) was introduced by cognitive psychologists Philip Gough and William Tunmer in 1986 and has become a cornerstone in literacy education. Their groundbreaking work provided a clear framework for understanding how reading comprehension develops. According to SVR, reading comprehension emerges from combining two essential skills: decoding (D) and language comprehension (LC). These components work together multiplicatively, as captured by the formula Decoding (D) × Language Comprehension (LC) = Reading Comprehension (RC).

Decoding

Decoding is the ability to translate written symbols into sounds—phonological awareness—supported by knowledge of how letters represent sounds. This skill enables readers to recognise words accurately and fluently, typically through phonics instruction. Decoding is the foundation of reading; without it, readers will likely struggle with comprehension.

Language comprehension

Language comprehension refers to the ability to understand spoken language, encompassing vocabulary, syntax and background knowledge, all of which contribute to making meaning of what is read. Even if a pupil is an excellent decoder, weak comprehension will lead to difficulties in understanding the text, as comprehension requires more than word recognition; it involves making inferences, connecting ideas and drawing on prior knowledge.

How decoding and language comprehension work together

The unique aspect of the Simple View is its multiplicative nature – both decoding and language comprehension must be strong for reading comprehension to flourish. If either component is weak, overall comprehension will suffer. A pupil who decodes well but lacks comprehension will still struggle with understanding the text, just as a pupil who understands language well but cannot decode will face similar challenges.

Empirical studies consistently support the SVR model. For example, Catts, Hogan and Fey (2003) found that both decoding and language comprehension predict reading comprehension in pupils across age groups. Similarly, Hoover and Gough (1990) showed that as decoding becomes automatic, language comprehension plays a larger role in understanding text. This shift illustrates how both components are crucial but change in importance as pupils develop.

Decoding
This fundamental reading skill involves translating written symbols (letters and words) into their corresponding sounds.

Teaching strategies for decoding and comprehension

The SVR offers clear guidance for reading instruction. Effective reading instruction needs to focus on both decoding and linguistic comprehension. Systematic phonics instruction is key to building decoding skills, while language comprehension requires exposure to rich oral and written language. Activities such as read-alouds, discussions and vocabulary-building exercises are crucial for expanding pupils' ability to understand language, especially as they move from learning to read to reading to learn.

Decoding should be explicitly taught through phonics, starting with basic letter-sound relationships, and advancing in complexity. Research has shown that teaching pupils how to decode words helps them become fluent readers. By developing automatic word recognition, pupils free up cognitive resources for comprehension.

Comprehension requires a broader instructional approach. Teachers can develop pupils' comprehension skills by fostering rich discussions, introducing complex vocabulary and encouraging oral language practice. Research highlights the importance of vocabulary in reading comprehension, making it essential to teach words in context and offer pupils a wide variety of texts.

Criticisms of the SVR

While the SVR has shaped reading instruction, it isn't without its critics. Some argue that it oversimplifies the reading process by overlooking factors such as motivation, metacognition and working memory. Reading is more than decoding and understanding; it involves monitoring one's comprehension and using strategies to overcome challenges. Scarborough's Reading Rope model (2001) (*see pages 14–17*) expands on the SVR by including background knowledge, verbal reasoning and word recognition, offering a more nuanced view.

Still, the SVR remains a powerful tool for understanding reading comprehension and emphasises the need for balance between decoding and language comprehension. Yet, as our understanding of literacy evolves, we must recognise that reading is a complex process that involves more than the components outlined in SVR. The future of literacy instruction will continue to integrate the SVR framework with broader theories and research, ensuring that all aspects of reading development are addressed in the classroom.

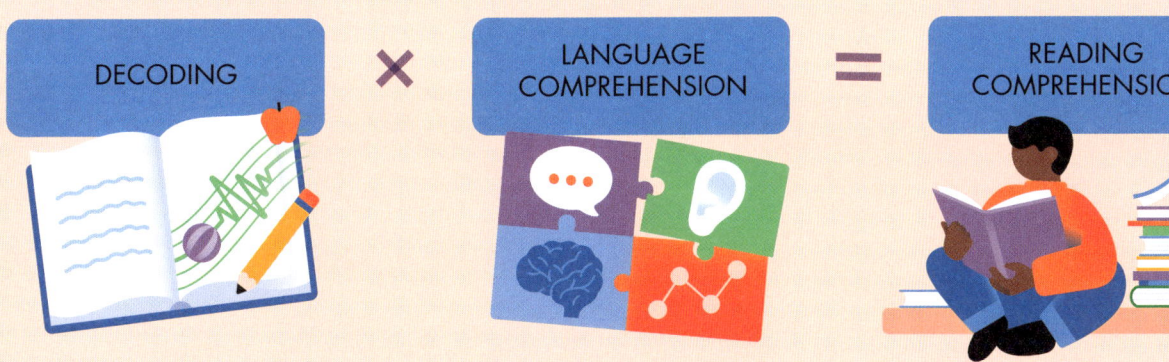

The Reading Rope

by Trina Gould Williams

The Reading Rope model is a visual representation created by Hollis Scarborough (2001). It represents subskills under the Word Recognition and Language Comprehension Domains that are needed to become a skilled reader.

Learning to read might seem simple, but it's quite a complex process that involves many different skills working together in the brain. Hollis Scarborough created the Reading Rope in 2001 to visually represent the subskills required for skilled reading. She described it as "an illustration of the many strands that are woven together in skilled reading", much like the instruments in an orchestra. Each subskill in the rope can function on its own, but together they create the "symphony" of a skilled reader.

The Reading Rope, the Simple View of Reading and their connection to the Science of Reading

The Simple View of Reading (SVR), introduced by researchers Gough and Tunmer (1986) and later expanded by Hoover and Gough (1990), explains the two main components necessary for reading:

Word recognition: the ability to decode words quickly and accurately

Language comprehension: the ability to understand spoken and written language

The SVR shows that skilled reading requires both components to work together. If either is missing (much like multiplying by zero), the result is incomplete comprehension. The Reading Rope builds on this concept by breaking down these two components into smaller, measurable skills that are critical for becoming a proficient reader by using a helpful metaphor of two strands of rope that twist together while learning to read. As readers develop both sets of skills, the strands become more tightly woven, forming a strong "rope" that helps them become skilled readers.

The top strand of the rope represents language comprehension, which is making meaning by understanding and interpreting the words of the text. The Reading Rope breaks this part of reading into five important areas:

Background knowledge: This is the information a reader already knows or learns about the topic they're reading. Background knowledge helps a child connect new information to what they already know, making comprehension easier.

Vocabulary: These are the words a reader knows and uses. Vocabulary grows when children hear and read more words, whether

"An illustration of the many strands that are woven together in skilled reading."

through conversation, books or even TV shows. A strong vocabulary helps readers grasp the meaning of texts as well as express themselves clearly.

Language structure: This covers the rules of grammar and how sentences are built, often called syntax. It also includes semantics, which is the meaning we get from how words are arranged in sentences.

Verbal reasoning: This is the ability to think through and interpret more complex ideas, such as making inferences or understanding the purpose behind a story.

Literacy knowledge: This is all the information readers learn about how books and written language work. It includes things like knowing that we read from left to right, that words are separated by spaces, and how to navigate a book (e.g., titles, chapters or pictures).

The bottom strand of the rope focuses on word recognition, which is essential for decoding text efficiently. Word recognition skills become more automatic as the reader continues to practise. This frees up mental energy for understanding the meaning of the text. The word recognition domain includes:

Decoding: The process of turning written letters into spoken words. It's a fundamental skill that helps readers figure out unfamiliar words.

Automaticity
As readers recognise words accurately and quickly, they free up mental energy for comprehension.

Phonological awareness: This refers to a reader's understanding of the sounds in words, helping readers connect spoken language to written language.

Sight recognition: As readers increase the volume of reading, they begin to recognise certain words instantly, without needing to sound them out.

The Science of Reading is not a specific programme or teaching method. Instead, it's a collection of research about how we learn to read. Tools like the Reading Rope and the Simple View of Reading are grounded in the Science of Reading. They guide educators and parents in understanding what children need to develop strong reading skills.

Scarborough's reading rope

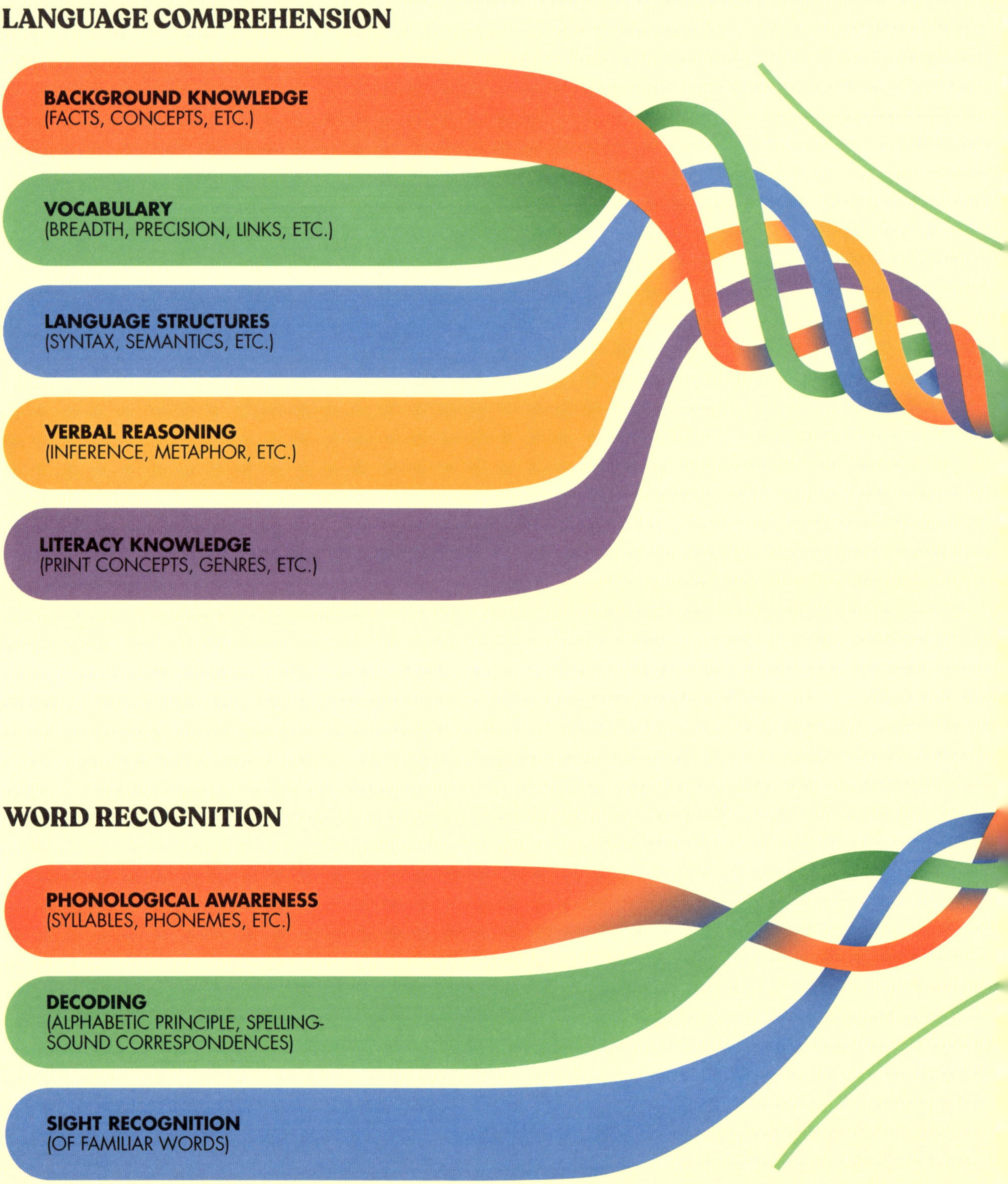

LANGUAGE COMPREHENSION

- **BACKGROUND KNOWLEDGE**
  (FACTS, CONCEPTS, ETC.)
- **VOCABULARY**
  (BREADTH, PRECISION, LINKS, ETC.)
- **LANGUAGE STRUCTURES**
  (SYNTAX, SEMANTICS, ETC.)
- **VERBAL REASONING**
  (INFERENCE, METAPHOR, ETC.)
- **LITERACY KNOWLEDGE**
  (PRINT CONCEPTS, GENRES, ETC.)

WORD RECOGNITION

- **PHONOLOGICAL AWARENESS**
  (SYLLABLES, PHONEMES, ETC.)
- **DECODING**
  (ALPHABETIC PRINCIPLE, SPELLING-SOUND CORRESPONDENCES)
- **SIGHT RECOGNITION**
  (OF FAMILIAR WORDS)

MODELS AND THEORIES OF READING 17

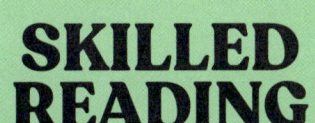

SKILLED READING
FLUENT EXECUTION AND COORDINATION OF WORD RECOGNITION AND TEXT COMPREHENSION

INCREASINGLY STRATEGIC

INCREASINGLY AUTOMATIC

How can parents support these skills?

Parents play a vital role in nurturing these skills at home. Engaging in meaningful conversations with your child can significantly enhance their language comprehension. The "Strive-for-Five" framework, for example, encourages parents to engage in back-and-forth conversations with their children, which can help develop vocabulary, verbal reasoning and language structures.

Reading aloud to your child is another effective way to support both word recognition and language comprehension. It exposes them to new vocabulary and language structures, while also allowing them to hear the sounds in words, which is essential for phonological awareness.

Understanding Reading Levels

by L. Crosby-Guard

Experts understand reading levels based on a child's skills and abilities, not necessarily the child's age or grade level. Learning about reading levels can help educators and families support children's literacy.

Proficient reading encompasses so many components and mitigating factors that there is not an exact correlation between age, grade and reading level. Ehri's phases provide a useful way of understanding children's reading levels.

Pre-alphabetic phase

This phase usually happens before children receive any formal reading instruction, which is typically at three or four years of age. Children in this reading phase do not understand the connection between letters, sounds and words. Instead, they will use context clues to guess what the words mean. One commonly observed behaviour is their ability to understand logos and signs, like a stop sign or the logo for a favourite shop or restaurant. The pre-alphabetic child cannot read, but they are smart and observant enough to memorise. Because of this reliance on memorisation, the pre-alphabetic child's spoken vocabulary can grow quickly, especially if they are read to regularly.

Partial alphabetic phase

Children transition to the partial alphabetic phase when they learn letters and the sounds that letters make. Children in the partial alphabetic phase cannot yet decode or sound out words because their alphabetic knowledge is simple. They can, however, hear phonemes, the smallest sounds in a word. Commonly, children in this phase might be asked to identify words that have the same beginning sound. ("*C* is for *cat*, /k/, *cat*. What are some other words that start with *c*?")

During instruction, they might be taught "word families" or words with similar middle and end phonemes but different beginning letters (such as *cat, fat, mat, sat*). Children can reach this phase between Reception and Year 1, but if older children have problems reading, they may struggle with the skills typical for this phase.

Alphabetic principle

As they learn to read, children understand the relationships between letters and sounds.

Full alphabetic phase

Increasing reading and writing instruction ushers children into the full alphabetic phase between first and second grade. Children in this phase are learning to associate letters, letter sounds and letter shapes as they write. They are learning to spell and decode words. In other words, phonics instruction has increased dramatically. Families may notice educators assign spelling tests and sight word lists. When children in the full alphabetic phase misspell, the errors are logical because they are based on phonological knowledge, such as *wus* instead of *was*. Again, struggling readers or children with reading abnormalities might get stuck in this phase, regardless of their grade level.

Consolidated alphabetic phase

As children practise reading, spelling and sounding out words, they move into the consolidated alphabetic phase. Children who have successfully transitioned to this phase recognise patterns in how words are spelled and pronounced. Common prefixes and suffixes make sense to them. Regular reading instruction and practice help children in this phase with fluency. Fluent readers can read with a natural flow and accuracy. They read faster, can decode multisyllabic words, can understand compound words and can use context clues to construct meaning. They understand text structures enough to aid their reading comprehension. In other words, they are learning to master words so well that they can start to focus on comprehending sentences and paragraphs.

Trying to learn, memorise and identify reading levels can quickly become overwhelming, but there is one easy thing that anyone can do to support children's literacy: read aloud. Read aloud to children. Have children read aloud. Reading aloud benefits children at every reading level.

Ehri's phases of reading development

CONSOLIDATED ALPHABETIC PHASE
TYPICAL AGE 6–8

Children can read faster and more easily. They understand word patterns and parts, such as prefixes and suffixes.

FULL ALPHABETIC PHASE
TYPICAL AGE 5–7

Children have an ability to decode regularly spelled words. They may make some spelling errors, but these are mainly logical errors based on phonological knowledge.

PARTIAL ALPHABETIC PHASE
TYPICAL AGE 4–6

Children have a partial understanding of letters and the sounds they make.

PRE-ALPHABETIC PHASE
TYPICAL AGE 3–4

Children cannot understand relationship between letters and sounds, but can use visual clues to recognise or guess words.

Foundational Reading Skills

The Critical Role of Phonemic Awareness	22
Phonological and Phonemic Awareness:	
Hearing All the Parts in a Word	26
Decoding the Mystery of Spelling	29
An Introduction to Phonics	32
Word Ladders for Decoding Instruction	36
Encoding and Literacy	38
Developing Children's Knowledge of Letters	40
High-Frequency Words and the Reading Journey	42
Word Recognition	46
Blending, Segmenting, Adding and Deleting Sounds	48
Rhyme Recognition	52

The Critical Role of Phonemic Awareness

by David D. Paige

Writing systems transform speech to text, with phonemes and graphemes forming the core of this process. English's complex structure, paired with phonemic awareness, plays a crucial role in learning to read.

Phonemic awareness helps pupils break down words like *cat* into individual sounds – /k/, /a/ and /t/.

Throughout history, writing systems have evolved to represent spoken language through symbols. Today, there are over 4,000 writing systems worldwide. English's intricate relationship between phonemes and graphemes presents challenges, especially for developing readers learning to decode words.

Text to speech

Writing is a system designed to convert speech to text. The oldest known writing system was created 5,200 years ago in what is now Iraq. Of the 7,000 languages in existence today, about 4,000 have a writing system.

Regardless of the language one speaks, each spoken word is composed of phonemes. A phoneme is the smallest unit of sound in speech. For example, when we pronounce the word *cat*, we quickly blend together three phonemes, /k/, /a/ and /t/. While there are about 800 phonemes across all languages, English uses 44. As an *alphabetic* writing system, English uses letters (called graphemes) to represent the 44 phonemes. Each of these graphophonic features is part of the English Alphabetic Code for converting text to speech, making graphemes and phonemes the nuts and bolts of written words.

The English Alphabetic Code

The English Alphabetic Code (*see pages 182–183*) refers to the system of representing the sounds (phonemes) of the English language with written letters or groups of letters (graphemes). This is the basis for reading and spelling in English. Phonic code tables for consonant sounds and vowel sounds are provided after this article.

Further, English is an opaque system, meaning how letters and phonemes are combined into sounds is not intuitive. When one can decipher the English Alphabetic Code, a process that takes most children several years, written words can be easily and quickly converted to speech. It is no surprise, then, that learning the English Alphabetic Code is the biggest challenge facing readers.

Phonemes

When a child begins to speak, their focus is on pronouncing the whole word. For example, the child learns to pronounce *frog* as a single speech unit, as they are unaware of the four phonemes comprising the word.

However, learning to pronounce a written word using phonic decoding is a completely different matter. Consider the six-letter word *freeze*, which is composed of four phonemes, /f/, /r/, /ē/ and /z/. The phoneme associated with a letter is most often not the letter name. To pronounce the phoneme /f/, we don't say "eeff",

we say the puff of air that is "fffffff". For /r/ we don't say "are," we say "ehrrr", and to pronounce /ē/ we say its name. The pronunciation of /z/ is "zzzzzz"; we do not add the phoneme "eee" at the end as we do to pronounce its name. To unlock a word from

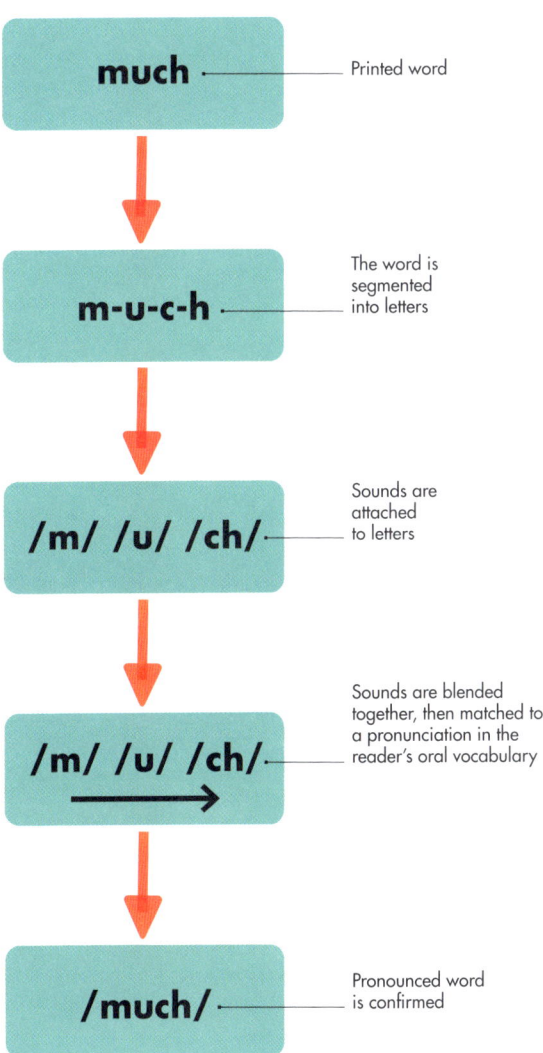

The phonic decoding process

- **much** — Printed word
- **m-u-c-h** — The word is segmented into letters
- **/m/ /u/ /ch/** — Sounds are attached to letters
- **/m/ /u/ /ch/** → — Sounds are blended together, then matched to a pronunciation in the reader's oral vocabulary
- **/much/** — Pronounced word is confirmed

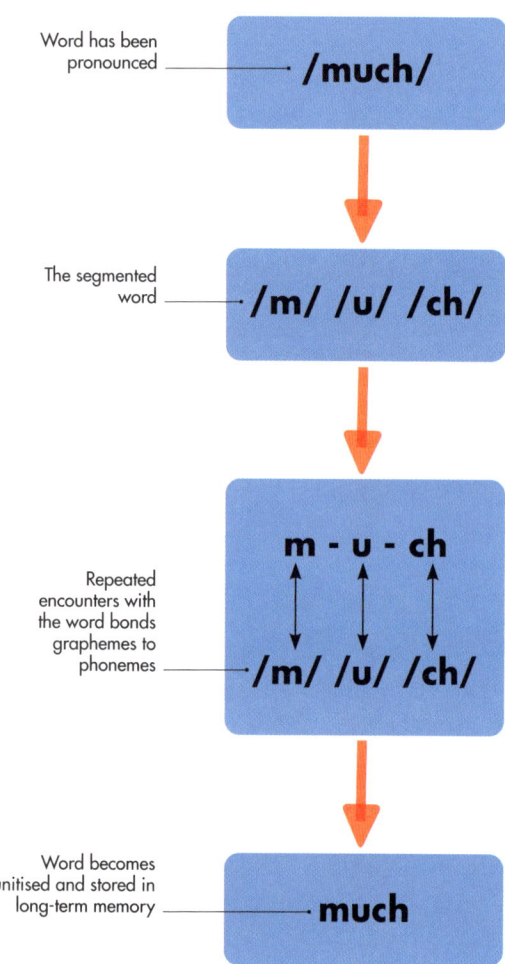

The process of orthographic mapping

- Word has been pronounced → /much/
- The segmented word → /m/ /u/ /ch/
- Repeated encounters with the word bonds graphemes to phonemes → m - u - ch ↕ /m/ /u/ /ch/
- Word becomes unitised and stored in long-term memory → much

> "Phonemic awareness instruction should be short, about five minutes a day."

print, the reader must be able to determine which letters are representing which of the 44 phonemes in English. While we are unaware of phonemes when we learn to speak, gaining awareness of them in print is, along with phonic decoding, critical to learning how to read words (Hulme et al., 2002; Treiman et al., 2019).

A child who has acquired phonemic awareness has the ability to aurally isolate, delete and replace a sound within a word to make a new word. Researchers have established that phonemic awareness is causal to reading acquisition and that its instruction has a significant impact on word reading (Hulme et al., 2012; Melby-Lervåg et al., 2012).

Orthographic mapping

The self-teaching hypothesis (Share, 1995, 1999) posits that to pronounce an unknown word, the reader uses their phonic decoding skills to segment the word into its individual phonemes, and then blend them into a pronunciation. Through this process, the pupil eventually learns to instantly recognise thousands of words. However, phonic decoding does not explain how a word becomes permanently stored in the reader's word inventory.

The orthographic mapping theory posits that phonemes become bonded to their written constituents along with the word's meaning, after one or several repetitions. This allows for storage of a high-quality, unitised lexical representation in the reader's long-term memory that becomes automatically activated upon recognition in text. For these connections to become automatised, the bonded, letter-to-sound connections must also be automatic.

Developing phonemic awareness

Importantly, it is not recognition of rhyming words, the clapping or tapping of syllables in a word, or even one's ability to segment and blend the sounds that predicts automatic word reading. Rather, it is phoneme manipulation skill (Dorofeeva et al., 2020; Kjeldsen et al., 2014; Savage & Carless, 2005). Further, Kilpatrick (2020) posits that it is instant phoneme manipulation skill that predicts automatic word reading. In other words, pupils who can instantly manipulate phonemes exhibit the underlying skill that is associated with automatic word reading. Aligned with this perspective are results from my own work (Paige, 2024). In a study of 160 first and second grade pupils, I compared untimed phoneme manipulation to instant manipulation (completed within two seconds). Results showed that instant manipulation, along with decoding knowledge, was a statistically significant predictor of automatic word reading while non-instant manipulation was not.

Assessing phonemic awareness

Remember that phonemic awareness is a cognitive activity that cannot be directly observed. However, a child can be asked to complete very carefully designed phoneme manipulation activities that indicate the extent to which the child possesses phonemic awareness. In 1963, D. B. Elkonin, a Russian psychologist, introduced the West to an instructional method that converted the abstract idea of phonemes into something much more concrete. Elkonin drew a simple rectangle on paper and divided it into four squares or boxes. Elkonin trained children to segment words based on their sounds by sliding a token for each sound into a box.

The box takes the abstraction of a phoneme and makes it more concrete. After children learn to segment words into sounds, they now have the prerequisite skills to learn how to substitute sounds to make new words. For example, the child might be told to use their Elkonin box to change the /ŏ/ sound in *dog* to /ĭ/, and then asked, "What is the new word?" (*dig*).

Phonemic awareness instruction

Phonemic awareness instruction should be short, about five minutes a day. Instruction should be conducted across Reception, understanding that the early part of the year will need to focus on learning alphabet knowledge that can be transitioned into sound blending. By later Reception, pupils who have mastered sound segmentation and blending can engage in phoneme manipulation. This instruction will likely continue into (and throughout) Year 1 for many pupils until sound manipulation is mastered.

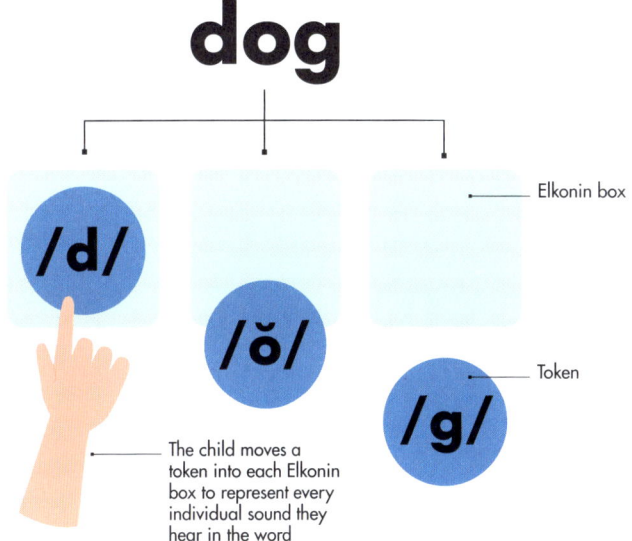

Mastery of aural, phoneme manipulation indicates that children have acquired the phonemic awareness skills necessary for orthographic mapping, which is critical to automatic word reading, to occur.

Phonological and Phonemic Awareness: Hearing All the Parts in a Word

by Bethanie Pletcher

Phonological and phonemic awareness predict success with decoding print. Educators and caregivers can use activities to help children build these skills.

Phonological awareness is the "awareness of sounds in words in learning to read and spell" (International Literacy Association, 2018). It encompasses the hearing of syllables (*cat-nip*) and onsets and rimes (*c-at*). Phonemic awareness is "the ability to detect and manipulate the smallest units (i.e., phonemes) of spoken language" (*c-a-t*) (International Literacy Association, 2018).

Because phonological and phonemic awareness predict success with decoding print, they also affect reading fluency and comprehension. Lundberg et al. (1988) asserted that early instruction in the areas of phonological and phonemic awareness has a substantial influence on reading and writing achievement. They also indicated that instruction should be explicit and fast-paced.

There exists a continuum of phonological and phonemic awareness skills, and caregivers should be cognisant of these because expecting a child to delete the initial sound

LESS COMPLEX TASK → **MORE COMPLEX TASK**

SENTENCE SEGMENTATION
Examples:
The/cat/is/furry.

ONSET AND RIME BLENDING AND SEGMENTING
Examples:
c-at

RHYMING AND ALLITERATION
Examples:
Rhyming: *cat/hat*
Alliteration: *cat/cup*

SYLLABLE BLENDING AND SEGMENTING
Examples:
cat/nip

INDIVIDUAL PHONEMES, INCLUDING IDENTITY, SEGMENTING, ADDITION, DELETION
Examples:
c-a-t

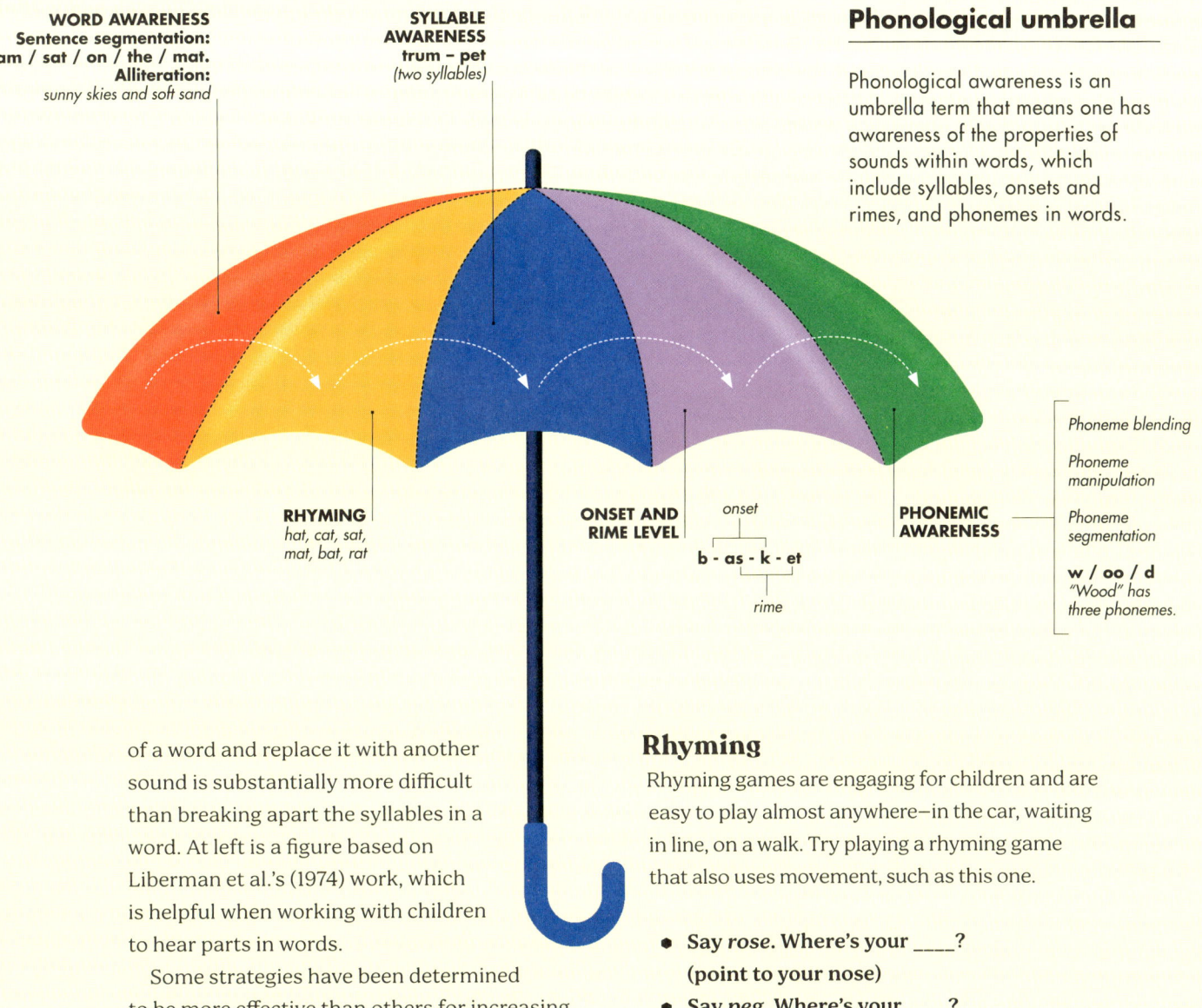

Phonological umbrella

Phonological awareness is an umbrella term that means one has awareness of the properties of sounds within words, which include syllables, onsets and rimes, and phonemes in words.

of a word and replace it with another sound is substantially more difficult than breaking apart the syllables in a word. At left is a figure based on Liberman et al.'s (1974) work, which is helpful when working with children to hear parts in words.

Some strategies have been determined to be more effective than others for increasing phonological and phonemic awareness, and more time should be spent on the far-right column of the continuum—working with individual phonemes (Reutzel, 2015). However, the concepts of rhyming, syllable blending and segmenting, and onset and rime blending and segmenting should still be addressed, as these are precursors to learning to work with phonemes. The following activities will help children learn these concepts.

Rhyming

Rhyming games are engaging for children and are easy to play almost anywhere—in the car, waiting in line, on a walk. Try playing a rhyming game that also uses movement, such as this one.

- Say *rose*. Where's your ____? (point to your nose)
- Say *peg*. Where's your ____? (point to your leg)
- Say *band*. Where's your ____? (point to your hand)

Repeat with different body parts.

Alliteration

Alliteration is when words begin with the same sound, like the words in a tongue-twister. One effective technique to teach children to hear words that begin with the same sound is to do a picture-sorting activity. All you will need are photographs or drawings of common objects (e.g., *bell, basket, car, cat, fish, fan, table, turtle*). First, have the child say the name of each item. Then, invite them to sort the pictures into pairs by which ones have the same first part. They should say the name of each picture again as they match the pairs.

Clapping syllables

Understanding how to break down words with more than one syllable is paramount, as this will help children write longer words and decode words while reading. Before using print, however, children need to be able to hear the larger parts of a word. An easy method to teach this is to invite them to clap the syllables in several words. Demonstrate by starting with their name —for example, *Lis-beth*. Then, move on to other words in which the syllables are clear. Begin with two-syllable words (*football, pumpkin*); then move on to three- (*banana, umbrella*) and four-syllable words (*watermelon*); and end with one-syllable words (*fork, rain*). The reason for clapping the syllable in one-syllable words last is because this can actually be more difficult than multisyllabic words as the child may anticipate that there is more than one syllable, mistakenly clapping *f-ork*.

Breaking words into onset and rime

After the child can hear the larger parts of words (syllables), it's time to move on to learning how to break them into smaller parts, such as onset and rime. The onset of a syllable includes all the consonants up until the first vowel. The rime of a word includes everything beginning with the first vowel. *Tap* contains the onset *t-* and the rime *-ap*. *Trip* contains the onset *tr-* and the rime *-ip*. Incorporate some movement into an activity for hearing onset and rime by demonstrating how you and the child can stand up when saying the onset and sit down when saying the rime.

Breaking words into their smallest parts

Hearing the smallest parts of a word, the phonemes, is the most challenging of the skills in the phonics skills continuum. One way to teach hearing phonemes is to use picture cards of one-syllable words that are cut into the number of phonemes they contain. For example, cut a picture of a hat into three pieces. As the child puts the pieces together, they will say the sounds, /h/-/a/-/t/. Demonstrate and repeat this process with other one-syllable words such as *fan* (/f/-/a/-/n/) and *lamp* (/l/-/a/-/m/-/p/).

Decoding the Mystery of Spelling

by Trina Gould Williams

Orthographic knowledge, or the "rules" that govern how we spell, isn't just about memorising spelling words. It also helps kids read.

Orthographic knowledge is simply our understanding of how letters and letter patterns represent sounds in written language. It's the "rules" (and delightful exceptions to those rules) that govern how we spell. It's not just about memorising; orthographic knowledge helps kids read.

Ever watched a child struggle over a seemingly simple word, sounding it out letter by agonising letter, only to get it wrong? Or maybe they can read a word one day and then misspell it the next? This common scenario highlights an example of orthographic knowledge. Think of it as the secret code of written English.

It's not just about memorising lists of words; it's about recognising patterns, understanding relationships between letters and sounds, and developing a visual memory for words.

So, how does this "secret code" help our kids become better readers? Let's break it down:

Beyond sounding out: While phonics (the relationship between sounds and letters) is essential for early reading, it's not the whole story. Orthography can either be shallow or transparent or deep or opaque. Transparent languages are characterised by each letter having its own distinct sound.

SOUNDS (PHONOLOGY)	MEANING	SPELLING (ORTHOGRAPHY)
		n**igh**t

English is a tricky language with many words that don't follow simple sound-letter correspondences. It is considered morphophonemic – the spelling represents both phonemes and morphemes. Think of words like *night*, *though* or *island*. Orthographic knowledge helps children recognise these irregular spellings and read them fluently. They're not just sounding out; they're recognising familiar letter patterns.

Building a mental dictionary: As children develop orthographic knowledge, they build a mental "dictionary" of familiar letter sequences and word patterns. These are sometimes referred to as "sight words". This allows them to recognise words quickly and effortlessly, freeing up mental energy to focus on comprehension. Imagine trying to read a sentence if you had to sound out every single word! It would be exhausting.

Predicting and confirming: Strong orthographic knowledge allows children to predict what a word might be based on its spelling patterns. When they encounter an unfamiliar word, they can use their knowledge of letter combinations and common spelling patterns to make educated guesses. Then, they can confirm their guess by checking the context of the sentence. This process of predicting and confirming enhances reading fluency and comprehension.

From reading to spelling (and back again): Reading and spelling are two sides of the same coin. As children become better spellers,

Children can use what they know about letters and sounds to determine the correct spelling of **regular** words, like *tin*.

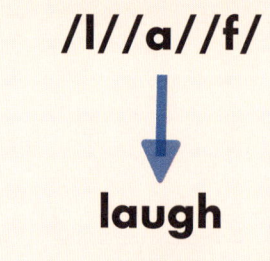

Some words, like *laugh*, have **irregular** spellings for certain sounds. Start by asking pupils to focus on parts of the word with regular spellings.

they also become better readers, and vice versa. When children learn to spell a word correctly, they're reinforcing their understanding of its letter patterns and visual form. This strengthens their ability to recognise the word when they encounter it in reading.

So, what can parents do to nurture their child's orthographic knowledge?

It's not about endless spelling tests! Here are some fun and engaging activities:

Word sorting: Sort words into categories based on spelling patterns (e.g. words with *ai*, words with *oa*). This helps children notice similarities and differences in spelling.

Word hunts: Go on "word hunts" in books or magazines, looking for words with specific spelling patterns. This makes learning interactive and engaging.

Playing word games: Word games are excellent for developing orthographic knowledge in a fun and competitive way.

Reading, reading, reading: The best way to develop orthographic knowledge is simply to read! The more children are exposed to written language, the more they will internalise spelling patterns and build their mental "dictionary" of words.

Focus on meaning: When discussing words with your child, don't just focus on the spelling.

Talk about the meaning of the word and use it in different contexts. This helps children connect the spelling to the meaning, making it more memorable.

In summary, orthographic knowledge is a vital component of reading that helps children recognise and understand words more efficiently. By understanding the "secret code" of written language, children can unlock the joy of reading and become confident, lifelong learners. It's not about rote memorisation; it's about fostering a deep understanding of how words work, one delightful letter pattern at a time.

An Introduction to Phonics

by Dr. Wiley Blevins

Phonics instruction teaches pupils how letters and sounds work together to form words. By understanding these relationships, learners develop essential decoding skills that build the foundation for fluent reading and effective comprehension.

Learning to read can feel almost magical as we transform those squiggles and lines on the page into words, sentences and ideas. But it's not magic. While our brains are wired to acquire speech naturally, reading is something that can and needs to be taught. The good news is that we have an alphabet to help us.

The English alphabet

English is an alphabetic language. The English alphabet has 26 letters. These letters, alone and in different combinations, can be used to represent the 44 sounds in English. For example, we can use the letter *b* to stand for the /b/ sound in a word like *ball* or the spelling *oa* to stand for the long *o* sound in *coat*.

What is phonics?

Phonics involves the teaching of the most common letter- or spelling-sound relationships. Once a beginning reader learns *s* for the /s/ sound, *a* for the /a/ sound, and *t* for the /t/ sound, that reader can decode (sound out) the word *sat*.

Understanding orthographic mapping

Sounding out helps us decode words, or lift them off the page to transform them into speech. When we sound out a word, we focus on the letters and sounds then attach the completed word to a meaning. This process is known as orthographic mapping *(see below)*. We must orthographically map words into memory in order to automatically retrieve them while reading. When we can do this, these words have become sight words. This enables our reading to be faster and more fluent.

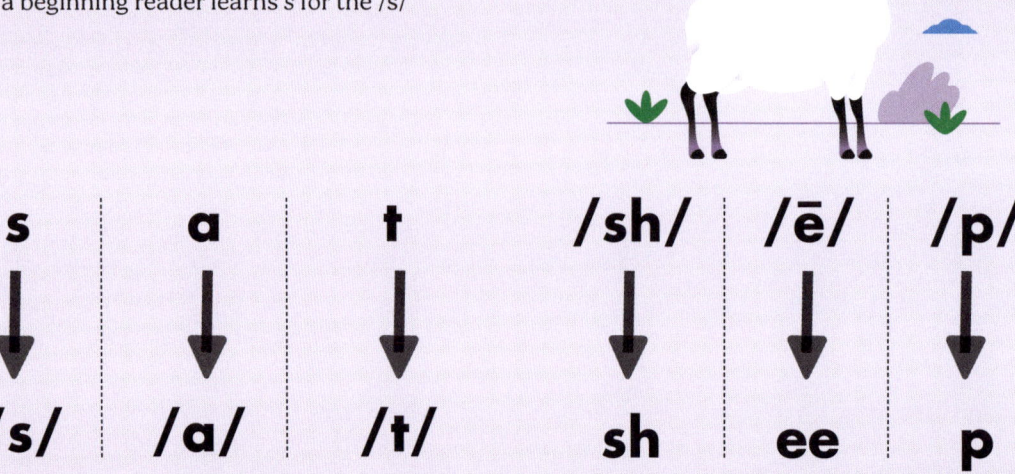

Difficulty with reading fluency can impact a pupil's entire literacy journey. When reading feels challenging, motivation drops, leading to less reading practice, a slower-growing vocabulary, and ultimately, limited comprehension. Addressing fluency early can help break this cycle and foster stronger, more confident readers.

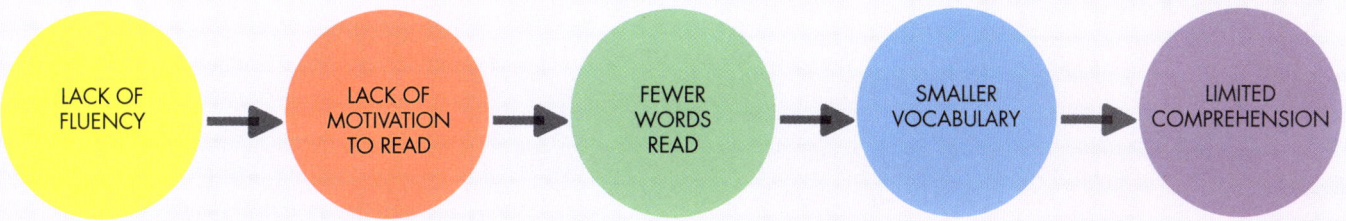

LACK OF FLUENCY → LACK OF MOTIVATION TO READ → FEWER WORDS READ → SMALLER VOCABULARY → LIMITED COMPREHENSION

Systemic and explicit instruction

Typically beginning readers are taught the most common spellings for each sound in the first two to three years of schooling. This instruction is best when it is explicit and systematic. After that, less common or more complex spellings are generally acquired though incidental learning.

Explicit instruction means that sound-spelling relationships like *sh* for the /sh/ sound and *ai* for the long *a* sound are taught directly to pupils rather than having them discover these connections.

Systematic means that the instruction has a clearly defined scope and sequence. (Scope is what will be taught, and sequence refers to the order it will be taught in.) While there is no agreed-upon scope and sequence, it is best to progress from easier to more complex skills and separate potentially confusing skills. A strong scope and sequence builds from the known to the new in easy steps that make the new learning more obvious and easier to grasp. It is also cumulative and recursive, systematically reviewing skills for many weeks after they have been taught to ensure they are mastered in both reading and writing. Young learners typically learn how to read words with new phonics skills faster than spelling words with those same skills. Thus, this extended learning is essential for spelling growth and fluency.

Building fluency through phonics

Fluency is the ultimate goal of phonics instruction. It is the automatic use of the skills in reading and writing. Fluency must be a focus of phonics instruction at the letter/spelling level, word level and connected text level. Without attention to fluency, pupils' reading can become slow and laboured, which negatively impacts comprehension.

To achieve maximum impact, phonics instruction must not be isolated from actual reading and writing practice. It is in the application of these skills where the learning sticks. The primary practice tool used during phonics instruction is the decodable reader, in which a high percentage of words can be fully sounded out based on the phonics skills taught up to that point. While there is no agreement on the actual percentage of words that need to be decodable, it is the intentionality and intensity of this practice that aid in building fluency.

ABOUT **84%** OF ENGLISH WORDS HAVE MOSTLY PREDICTABLE SPELLING PATTERNS, MAKING THE LEARNING OF PHONICS A **POWERFUL TOOL** FOR READING

Decodable text

Decodable text is a powerful tool in early literacy, connecting the dots between phonics and fluency, comprehension, vocabulary and writing skills.

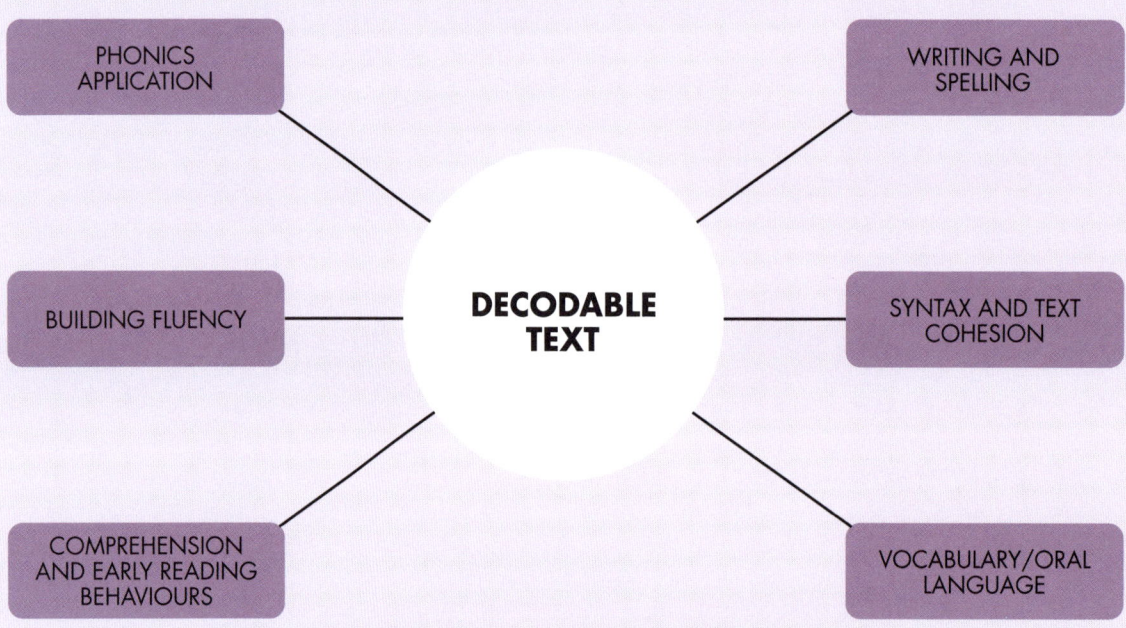

From building fluency to enhancing syntax and text cohesion, decodable books reinforce foundational reading behaviours, creating a cohesive map that supports children on their journey from decoding words to understanding meaning.

The role of decodable texts

Young readers engage with decodable texts when first introduced to a new phonics skill to practise using it to read words in connected text. They then reread these texts multiple times to become fluent with the skill. The large number of words with the new phonics skills in these texts builds statistical awareness of common spelling patterns and their position in words (e.g., *ai* in the middle of words and *ay* at the end: *rain/play*), which aids in spelling development. Therefore, this practice tool is essential for decoding, fluency and spelling development. In addition, this instructional tool can and should be used to build early reading behaviours, develop comprehension and include vocabulary instruction. It also serves as a springboard for writing and spelling work while addressing issues pupils might have with text cohesion and sentence syntax.

Decodable texts are not the only texts pupils should encounter in early reading instruction. They must also be simultaneously exposed to more complex texts that are designed to build vocabulary and content knowledge through read-alouds and rich conversations about these texts. Reading involves more than decoding words on a page; it also involves knowing the meanings of those words and connecting the ideas in the texts to previous learning.

Although English is a more opaque, or complex, language than others (for example, Spanish), a high percentage of English words can be read and spelled using deep knowledge of how English words work. Phonics instruction serves that vital role.

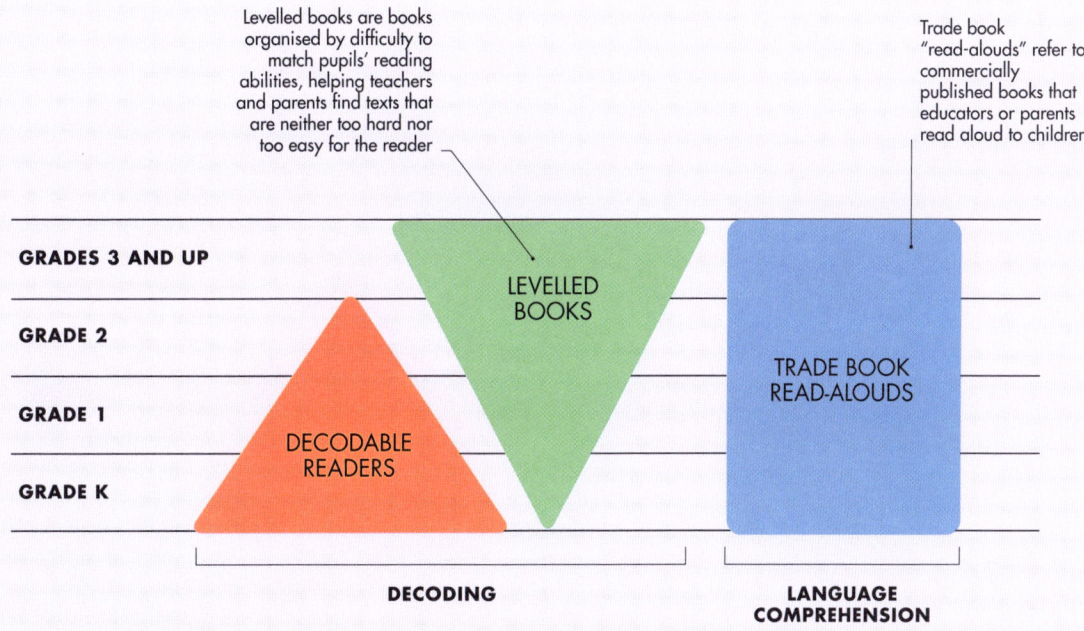

Word Ladders for Decoding Instruction

by Timothy Rasinski, PhD

Phonics is crucial for pupils' reading success. Word ladders are one effective strategy for learning how to decode words.

We are in a critical period with regard to literacy development and instruction. In the United States, over the past 20+ years, despite enormous efforts by the federal government, individual states, school districts, individual schools, principals, teachers and parents, we have seen virtually no progress in improving reading outcomes. Indeed, a 2022 report by the US Department of Education found that about two-thirds of fourth-grade pupils (9- to 10-year olds) are reading at a level either at or below "basic" (National Center for Education Statistics, National Assessment of Educational Progress, 2022).

The Science of Reading movement has attempted to shed light on the lack of progress in pupils' reading achievement by focusing on reading competencies that have been validated through scientific research. One of those competencies is word decoding or phonics. And one instructional approach that has been found to be effective goes by several names: word building, word chains or word ladders.

Word building
Creating words helps pupils with fluency, decoding and vocabulary.

Using word ladders and other word games

In a word ladder, pupils start with one word and are then guided by a teacher to go from one word to the next by adding, subtracting or changing one or a few letters (and sounds) from the previous word.

A game-like feature of many word ladders is that the first and last words in the ladder are somehow related. This game-like nature of many word ladders adds to the engagement of the activity for pupils. How many of us adults enjoy playing word games such as Scrabble® or Wordle alone or with friends? Note also that when playing word games on a regular basis, we become better at the game as we discover more fully how words are made. And we have a special name for such discoveries – learning! In a similar way, when pupils engage in word game activities, they too learn more deeply how words work.

Benefits of constructing and playing with words

Indeed, in doing word ladders regularly, pupils gain insights into word construction, word decoding, word encoding (spelling) and vocabulary (as the teacher can add meaning-based clues when guiding pupils from one word to the next). Scientific research has shown that children identified as struggling with word decoding demonstrated significant improvements in phonological awareness, word decoding and reading comprehension when engaged in word ladder instruction in just 20 lessons (McCandliss et al., 2003). When pupils are able to decode, encode and understand the meaning of words, overall reading achievement is bound to improve. Word ladders are one proven way to make this happen.

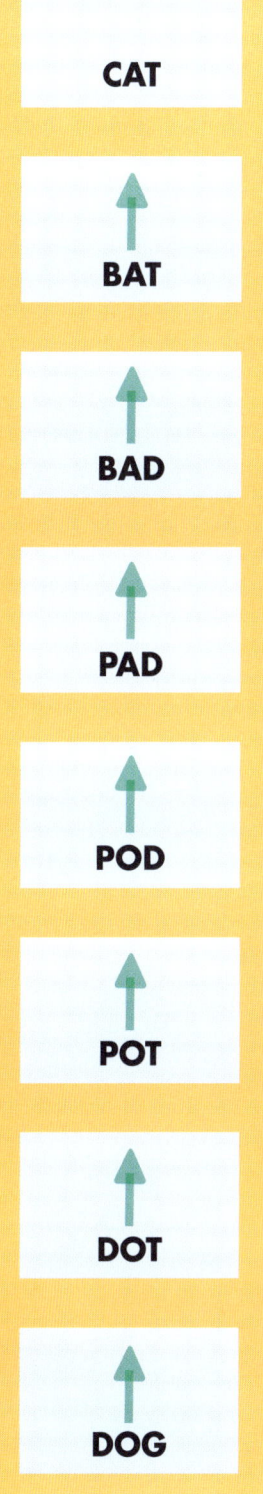

Encoding and Literacy

by Bethanie Pletcher

For many children, learning to write is the key that unlocks the world of print. Effective strategies can make children more comfortable with the writing process.

Some may say writing is easy – just grab a pen or pencil and put some words on paper, right? But it was only about 5,500 years ago that humans began creating print, a small amount of time relative to our existence.

Before that time, humans communicated through oral language. Consider everything we have to know to produce a message. First, we must think of what we want to write. Is it an email? A story? Next, we must organise our writing and envision what it will look like on paper or on the screen. Then we must think of the words we want to write and form or type each letter, one at a time.

What is encoding?

Now think about this whole process through the eyes of a young child, age five or six. That last step mentioned above is called encoding. The child has to construct a word by saying it (most likely saying it aloud so they can hear all the sounds), thinking about which sounds are in the word, matching each of those sounds with a letter (or more than one letter) and then forming that letter on paper. Whew! What strategies can caregivers use to help a child orchestrate these skills smoothly and automatically?

It's important to understand that reading, writing, spelling, phonemic awareness and phonics are connected (Graham & Hebert, 2011). This means that early writers are still learning

"Reading, writing, spelling, phonemic awareness and phonics are connected."

about letters and sounds. Reading and writing longer messages will help them solidify this information so that they can become fluent in both tasks, without having to slow down and attend to spelling words (Wyse & Hacking, 2024). For example, when a young child is reading a text out loud and comes to a difficult word, a caregiver can say, "Let's write that word and say the sounds as we write it." This strategy, called Write It Out (Stouffer, 2023), helps the child say the parts of the word in order, slowing down to write the letters that represent those parts. The following two activities can also help the child develop these skills.

Sound boxes and letter boxes

Elkonin boxes, or sound boxes, allow children to hear phonemes in words. A phoneme is the smallest sound we can hear in a word. For example, the word *dog* has three phonemes – /d/, /o/ and /g/, and the word *chip* also has three phonemes – /ch/, /i/, /p/. For this activity, you will need a piece of paper, a marker and pennies or buttons. Use these steps:

Model saying the word slowly and naturally and invite the child to do the same. Try the following words for practice: *egg, pie* (two phonemes), *fan, pig, sock* (three phonemes) and *lamp* and *nest* (four phonemes). Draw a box for each phoneme in the word.

Demonstrate pushing a penny or button in a box for each phoneme, saying, "I push in a penny/button each time I hear a sound". Try sharing the task by saying the word as the child pushes the pennies/buttons and having the child say the word while you push the pennies/buttons. Once this process is easy for the child, add a letter or letters to the boxes for each sound that is heard.

Interactive writing

Interactive writing is another powerful teaching strategy, in which the caregiver and the child write meaningful, co-constructed messages using a "shared pen" technique. First, talk with the child about a recent shared experience, such as a trip to the grocery store. Next, come up with a sentence or two to write about the shared experience. Allow the child to put the sentence in their own words. Then write the message, inviting the child to write what they can. You may write anything the child is not yet ready to write. When the message is complete, reread it with the child and invite the child to read it independently. Write the message on a different piece of paper and cut the words apart while the child reads them. Then mix up the words and invite the child to put them back together.

Conclusion

Becoming literate is about learning to write, not just learning to read. These strategies can help a child feel comfortable putting their ideas on paper and sharing them with others.

Developing Children's Knowledge of Letters

by Bethanie Pletcher

For the reading process to function, letter recognition needs to be automatic. Teachers and caregivers can use strategies to support this process.

Knowledge of the alphabet is "the recognition and naming of uppercase and lowercase letters and the paired associations between letter names and letter sounds" (Invernizzi & Buckrop, 2018, p. 86), as well as being able to form letters. This is a big task, as there are 40 distinctive shapes in letters to learn and children need to be able to automatically identify letters both in isolation and while reading and writing text. One important thing to remember is that children can learn about letters while learning to read and write. According to Clay (2005), there are three ways to "know" a letter: by its name, by its sound or by a word beginning with the letter.

Why is it important to teach (and continue to teach) letters?

Children need to recognise letters fluently. Adams (1990), in her book *Beginning to Read: Thinking and Learning About Print*, made it clear that letter recognition must be automatic for the reading process to function; otherwise, readers read one letter at a time, which makes fluent reading impossible. Prior to Adams's book, Rumelhart and McClelland (1986) developed a model of reading in which the reader recognises print at the letter level, by intaking the lines, curves and angles of letters. The more exposure to print the reader has, the more efficiently this process works.

Letter knowledge
Children know a letter's name, its sound and a word starting with the letter.

In what order should letters be taught?

The letters in each child's name should be taught first, as children are quicker to learn letters that are meaningful to them (Treiman & Broderick, 1998). Also, teachers should consider how often the letters appear in text (Invernizzi & Buckrop, 2018). For example, *s*, *t*, *e* and *m* appear more frequently than *x* and *z*. Placement in the alphabet also makes a difference. Justice et al. (2006) found that children are more likely to learn the letters near the beginning of the alphabet (*a, b, c, d, e*) first. Children also learn the letters whose sound is similar to the letter name faster than they learn the letters whose sounds are quite different from their names. For example, when pronounced, the letter *b* has the

/b/ sound, but the letter *w* when pronounced does not contain the sound that *w* makes in most words (Treiman & Broderick, 1998).

What are some research-based strategies for working with letters?

Consistent practice and rehearsal are needed to ensure fluency and overlearning (Ehri & Roberts, 2006). Also, informal experiences with letters are just as important as formal ones. These include singing the alphabet song, writing names and noticing letters in the child's environment.

Some materials can make letter learning novel and fun. Magnetic letters are colourful and tactile, allowing children to get to know letters' shapes and features. Surfaces such as small dry-erase boards and chalkboards can help children practise writing letters.

Sample activities

- **Match magnetic letters to letters written on bingo cards.**
- **Have children run their fingers over magnetic letters.**
- **Talk about the similarities and differences of capital and lowercase forms of letters.**
- **Model the formation of a new letter on a writing surface. Talk about your movements (for example, "around, up and down" for the letter *d*).**
- **Guide children's hands as they write the letter.**
- **Invite children to write the letter on different surfaces and in different sizes.**
- **Sort, sort, sort! There are many ways to sort letters (letters with short sticks/tall sticks; letters with tunnels and letters with circles).**

Letter Sorting

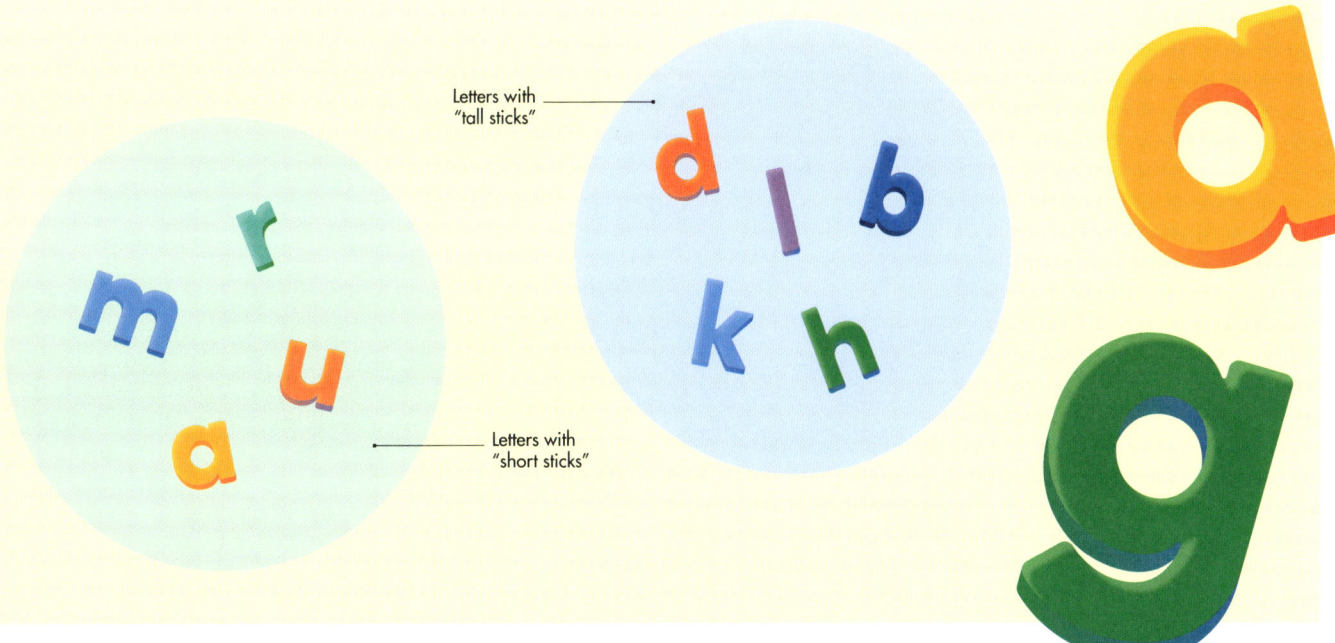

High-Frequency Words and the Reading Journey

by Jake Downs

High-frequency words are everywhere. How can educators best help pupils understand and read them?

High-frequency words (HFWs) refer to the most common words in the English language. Teachers can refer to several lists of common words, such as the Dolch (1936) and Fry (1980) lists, which share many of the same words. Early reading instruction often prioritises these high-frequency words because they significantly impact early reading. For example, the 100 most frequent words account for roughly 50% of written English (Green et al., 2024). This means that by mastering these 100 words, pupils can significantly improve their overall reading accuracy and comprehension from the very beginning of their reading journey. But HFWs have different traits. By recognising different types of HFWs, educators can use effective strategies for teaching them.

Teaching high-frequency words

A common approach to teaching HFWs involves daily instruction, typically including both the introduction of new words and the review of previously learned ones. Crucially, all HFW practice should include practice in connected text using productive fluency practices. Teachers wishing to make their instruction more efficient could survey pupils' accuracy in the most frequent 100 words several times per year. A parent volunteer, student teacher or paraprofessional could easily assist in this process. The resultant data would illuminate which words pupils need the most help with and which words could consume little – or no – instructional time.

Teaching different types of high-frequency words

Type	Short regular words	Short irregular words	Longer words
Examples	it can yes	one come does	because different myself
How to teach them	Encourage pupils to apply phonics skills to sound out the words.	Use activities to help pupils memorise these words.	Use strategies to break the words into syllables.

High-frequency word considerations

When teaching HFWs, it's crucial to consider factors that influence their difficulty, such as regularity in spelling-sound correspondence, word length and morphological structure. Short, phonetically regular words such as *at*, *will*, *up* and *did* are generally easier to decode Instruction for these words may require less dedicated time and can often be integrated into the regular phonics curriculum (Fuchs et al., 2024).

Many HFWs have some degree of irregularity in their spelling-sound correspondence. While some, such as *is* or *from*, have minor irregularities (e.g. the *s* in *is* is pronounced as /z/), others, such as *could*, are more irregular. Irregular words can be challenging for pupils to read because they don't follow the most common rules of phonics. To effectively learn these words, it's crucial to implement specific instructional routines such as "heart words" or "mispronunciation correction" (Colenbrander et al., 2022). These routines help pupils learn the unique spellings and pronunciations of irregular words through repeated exposure and practice, ultimately leading to accurate and automatic word recognition. Due to their irregular nature, these words may require more instructional time compared to short, regular words.

Importantly, the top 100 HFWs contain mostly short regular and short irregular words. Still, a minority of HFWs are longer or contain suffixes which bear instructional consideration. Longer HFWs may add additional challenges to decode, but not always. For instance, the HFW *number* is one of the longest in the top 100 HFWs, but would be considered regular. Syllabication or long-word reading strategies (*see pages 82–84*) could be employed when learning bisyllabic HFWs.

Added morphology

Last, a limited number of HFWs contain suffixes—such as *its*, *called* and *words*. These words and others also could readily include added suffixes to create words not on the HFW list, such as adding the suffix *-ly* to the HFW *time*. This provides an excellent opportunity to introduce morphological features to pupils. Additionally, suffixes such as *-s* and *-ed* can vary in their pronunciation (/s/ and /z/ for *-s*, and /ed/, /d/ and /t/ for *-ed*), which may offer additional opportunity for practice using irregular word strategies.

Conclusion

The most frequent 100 words in English comprise roughly 50% of written text. These high-frequency words vary in their regularity, length and morphology features, which should influence the approaches teachers employ for instruction. Efficiently and effectively learning these words may provide pupils with an early benefit in reading.

The 100 most frequent words account for about 50% of written English.

"A high percentage of English words can be read and spelled using deep knowledge of how English words work."

Wiley Blevins

Word Recognition

by Megan Meade

Can you imagine sounding out every word in a long novel? Reading would be a laborious and difficult endeavour. This is where word recognition comes in to save the day.

Word recognition is the ability to look at a word and automatically identify what it is. This is a word that a reader has seen so many times that they no longer have to pause to sound it out.

The importance of word recognition

Word recognition helps a reader excel in several areas: fluency, comprehension and confidence.

A fluent reader is one who reads with accuracy and expression, as if they are speaking conversationally. Reading fluently will increase a reader's comprehension of the text. Readers will be able to better absorb the story and its characters in fictional works or the information and its main ideas in nonfiction. Lastly, word recognition builds a reader's confidence. People enjoy doing things that they are good at, and young readers are no different. And as we all know, the more practice a person engages in, the more their skills sharpen.

Encouraging word recognition in young readers

Here are some common ways to expand a reader's exposure to words in their everyday routine.

High-frequency words: Lists of high-frequency words are made up of the most commonly used words (e.g., *the, be, to*) in the English language. By reviewing these words frequently, readers will automatically recall them when they encounter the words in text. When possible, make sure readers understand that some sight words can be "sounded out" phonetically (e.g. *it, not, on*). Other words do not follow standard phonetic rules (e.g. *the, of, have*).

Word walls and other text-rich environments: In classrooms, you can provide pupils with a Word Wall to display frequently used words they can reference easily. Alternatively, any room can be turned into a text-rich environment by labelling items inside of it. For instance, if a box of tissues is labelled with the word *tissue*, a reader will see that word each time they walk up to the box. They will begin to automatically associate the word's visual with the item that it is written on. To level up the effectiveness of a text-rich environment, use it as a living game board, asking readers to find certain words in the room.

> "Word recognition is the ability to look at a word and automatically identify what it is".

The twenty most common words in the English language

Reviewing lists of high-frequency words helps readers recall them when they read.

Recognising words while reading:
Consider choosing a specific topic with common vocabulary words to study more in-depth. Visit the local or school library to check out related books. Each time the reader comes across common words (such as *cat, kitten, milk, meow, hiss*), ask the reader to read it aloud. As they read through the texts and gain repeated exposure to the words, they should begin recalling them automatically.

Think of word recognition in terms of learning a new language. At first, it's very difficult to follow along because you need to translate each word into English in your mind. Eventually, you no longer have to do that, and it becomes easier to understand your new language. Word recognition in phonics instruction is just a different application of this same concept.

Blending, Segmenting, Adding and Deleting Sounds

by Megan Meade

Chances are, you've heard the colloquial way of referring to the skill of decoding unfamiliar words: "sounding it out". Phoneme manipulation – through blending, segmenting, adding and deleting sounds – provides a useful strategy for decoding words.

Every reader's skill set starts with learning the letters and sounds of the alphabet. Once they can do so with ease, they can move onto blending those sounds together to form a word. For instance, the word *cat* is made up of three letter sounds, /k/ /ă/ /t/, that the reader would then blend together, /kăt/. This is what is often referred to as "sounding it out". Of course, readers can reverse engineer this skill, segmenting the word *cat* into its individual sounds, /k/ /ă/ /t/, which is an important pre-spelling skill.

Deletion (and its related opposite, addition) is a similar skill where a reader manipulates a word by removing or adding a sound and recognising the word that is left behind. An example of this is when a pupil is reading the word *snap*, drops the /s/ and decodes the leftover word as *nap*.

The importance of manipulating sounds

Readers who blend, segment, add and delete sounds with ease have a strong phonemic awareness, which is a reader's ability to hear and work with different sounds (*see pages 22–23*).

Think of it as cracking a code. The alphabet and its associated sounds are the code. Readers take this code and apply it to any given word. At first, they start by deciphering the sounds and identifying the word. Then they can work backward, pulling the sounds from the words. Eventually, they work with the code themselves, manipulating the words using deletion and addition techniques, and eventually in their very own writing.

Encouraging phoneme manipulation

There are a variety of ways that a reader can practise these important skills in the classroom or at home. Three of the simplest but most effective ways to do this are word studies, word families and word chaining.

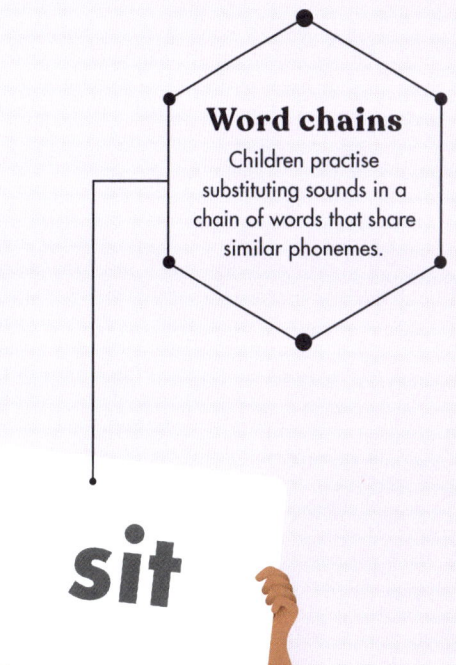

Word chains
Children practise substituting sounds in a chain of words that share similar phonemes.

Word study: This activity can be done to specifically target blending, segmenting or deleting, and you can use anything from alphabet books to magnetic letters on white/chalkboards. To practise blending, you visually provide a word and ask pupils to sound out the word and then blend it together. To practise segmenting, you verbally provide a word and ask them to identify each letter based on the sounds they hear. Lastly, to practise deletion and addition, you can tell them to remove a sound, possibly replacing it with another sound, aiding them in manipulating the word according to your direction.

Word families: Word families are groups of words that share a common ending, such as the *-at* family (*bat*, *cat*, *mat*, *sat*) or the *-ig* family (*big*, *dig*, *fig*, *wig*). These groups help readers recognise a common pattern (*-at* or *-ig*) that they can use to decode words more quickly. To practise recognising patterns, you can use magnetic letters or a white/chalkboard to show how the last two letters always stay the same, but by changing the first letter(s), you can change the word entirely. With practice, readers will realise that once they recognise a word family pattern, they no longer need to sound out each sound and can speed the decoding process along.

Word chaining: This activity has a simple premise with endless possibilities. First, you ask your reader to write a word such as *map*, helping them segment the sounds if necessary. Then, ask the child to change one sound into another, such as the /p/ into a /t/, to create a new word (*mat*). After they identify the new word, instruct them to change another sound, such as changing the /m/ to a /k/ to create a third word (*cat*). This can be done indefinitely.

Reading does not have to be a big mystery for young readers. When given the code and shown how to crack it, readers can quickly excel at not just decoding words but also using the code to create their own!

Manipulating phonemes gives children practise that helps them "sound out" words when they read.

Activities for adding, deleting and substituting sounds

Phoneme manipulation through adding, deleting and substituting sounds helps children develop key skills. By breaking down words and constructing new ones, they learn how to recognise individual sounds and read with automaticity.

ADDING PHONEMES

INITIAL PHONEME
Start with the word *ate*. Add /l/ to the beginning to make *late*.

ate
↓
late

FINAL PHONEME
Start with the word *pin*. Add /k/ to the end to make *pink*.

pin
↓
pin**k**

DELETING PHONEMES

INITIAL PHONEME
Start with the word *band*. Take away /b/ from the beginning to make *and*.

band
↓
and

FINAL PHONEME
Start with the word *past*. Take away /t/ from the end to make *pass*.

pas**t**
↓
pass

SUBSTITUTING PHONEMES

INITIAL PHONEME
Start with the word *brick*. Change the /b/ to a /t/ to make *trick*.

brick
↓
trick

MIDDLE PHONEME
Start with the word *fin*. Change the /i/ to an /a/ to make *fan*.

f**i**n
↓
f**a**n

FINAL PHONEME
Start with the word *thick*. Change the /k/ to an /n/ to make *thin*.

thi**ck**
↓
thi**n**

SCAFFOLDING THE ACTIVITIES

Start with simple VC words with only two phonemes, such as *in* and *at*. Move on to CVC words like *cap*, *in* and *pet*, as well as CV words like *go* and *be*. Introduce split vowel (silent *e*) words such as *gate*.

As children become more comfortable with the activity, use words with initial and final adjacent consonants such as *belt*, *smile*, *grant* and *mist*.

Next, move on to words with digraphs and trigraphs, such as *shin*, *bench* and *patch*.

Rhyme Recognition
by Megan Meade

"Twinkle, twinkle, little star, how I wonder what you are!" Nursery rhymes are some of the oldest ways that people teach young children. So why is rhyming so effective?

What is rhyme recognition?

Rhyme recognition is the ability to recognise that two different words end with the same sound, such as *cat* and *sat*. Most words that young children are exposed to have an **onset** and **rime**. This is a rudimentary way to break up words, common with young children. The onset is the first part of a word, such as /k/ in *cat* or /spl/ in *splat*. The rime is the rest of the word, which would be /at/ in both *cat* and *splat*. A child determining what words rhyme with them may break up a word such as *sat* into the onset and rime /s/ /at/, to compare their rimes.

This skill usually starts developing around ages three or four. You'll notice that children not only recognise rhyming words but they can produce their own rhyming pairs using both real and nonsense words.

Why is rhyme recognition important?

Rhymes help young readers develop an awareness of the sounds within words. In "Twinkle, Twinkle", a child will hear a variety of rhymes (*star/are*, *high/sky*) as the song is sung. This shows the child that many different words can have similar, smaller sounds within them.

Repeated exposure to rhyming words starts establishing patterns in their young minds. These patterns will become more formalised when they are introduced to word families (such as the *-at* word family, made up of words like *bat*, *cat*, *hat*, *sat*) early in their academic careers.

Rhyming, whether it is in a song or a book, is often repetitive. This makes rhymes deeply memorable to young audiences, further strengthening those neural pathways in developing brains. This not only lays the foundation for learning but is also fun and engaging for younger children.

Eventually, this onset/rime chunking will morph into the ability to hear each individual sound in a word when beginning readers start "sounding out" words.

How can you encourage rhyme recognition?

It is never too early to expose a child to rhyming. While an infant listening to a caregiver sing "Twinkle, Twinkle" is not identifying rhyming words, the foundations for those patterns are being laid. As children move through their early schooling, they will benefit greatly from the following rhyming activities:

- **singing rhyming songs, such as nursery rhymes**
- **reading rhyming books, such as many stories in Dr. Seuss's collection or *Brown Bear, Brown Bear, What Do You See?* by Bill Martin, Jr.**
- **playing rhyming games, such as education puzzles that focus on rhyming**
- **exploring word families, such as the *-at*, *-ed*, *-ig*, *-od* or *-un* families**

Rhyming words in a word family

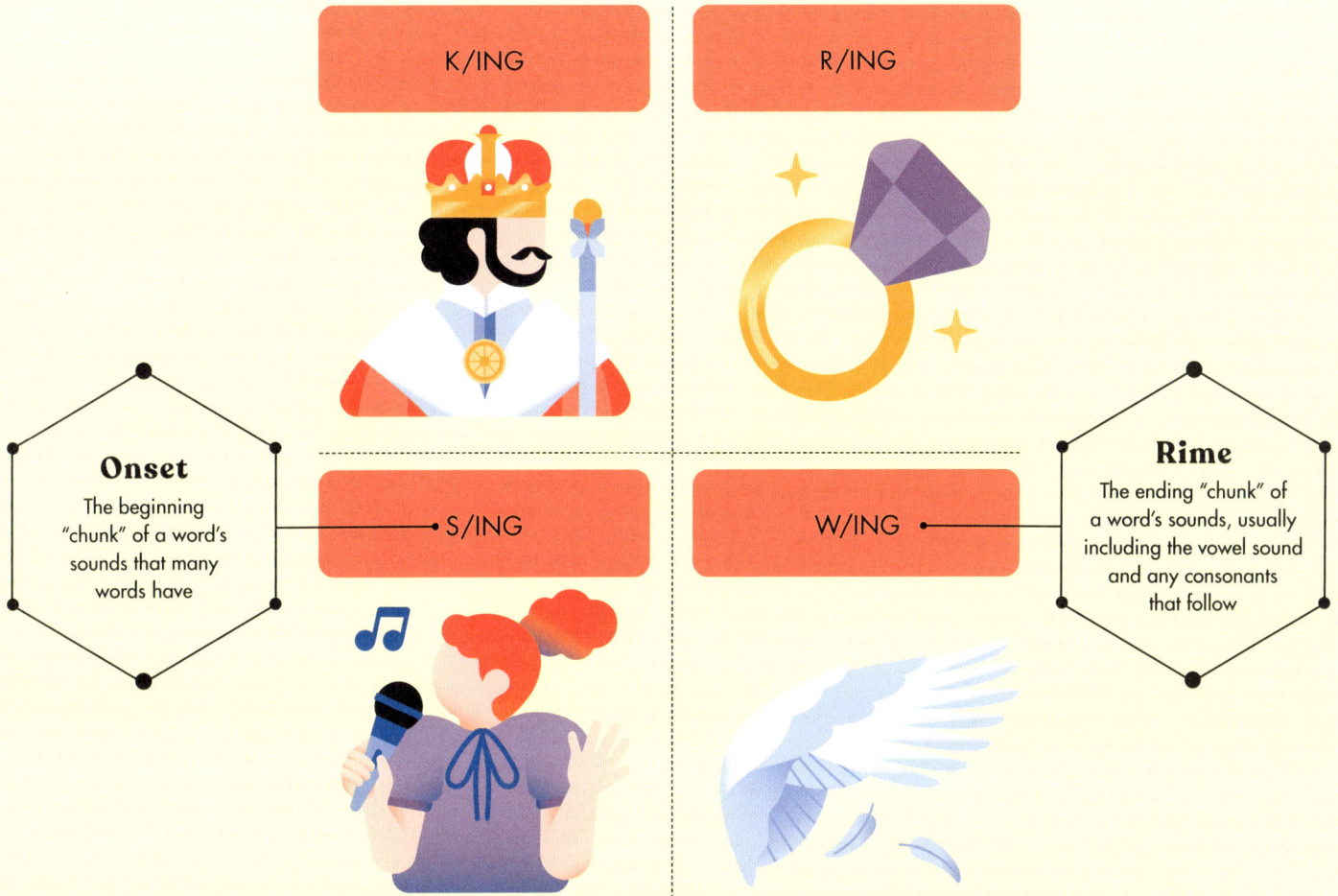

When exploring these mediums, it is helpful to highlight the rhyming words with your voice to draw attention to them ("Twinkle, twinkle, little **star**; How I wonder what you **are**!") as children begin to get comfortable with the skill.

If they still struggle, you can pull the words out once you are done reading by asking if each pair rhymes (*star/are?*). Pulling the words out as pairs puts them next to each other, helping children identify if they rhyme without the rest of the sentence cluttering their thought process.

If a reader is advancing past this, consider asking them to fill in the blank for the second word in each pair or come up with other words that rhyme with the pair. This will let them flex their mental muscles independently.

Rhyming is an important pre-reading skill that pays dividends when pupils first arrive at school. Early reading mainly focuses on understanding how sounds make up words and the patterns they can follow.

Advanced Reading Skills and Strategies

Reading Fluency	56
Research-Backed Ways to Teach Vocabulary	60
Independent Reading	63
Developing Deep Understanding Through Close Reading	66
Interrupted Reading	68
Sharing Text with Paired Oral Reading	70
Reading Motivation	76
Reading Engagement	78
Reading Multisyllabic Words	82
Repeated Reading	85

Reading Fluency

by Jan Hasbrouck, PhD

Reading fluency is essential for comprehension, but it's often misunderstood as merely reading fast. This article defines fluency, explores its components – accuracy, rate and expression – and offers strategies for assessing and teaching it effectively.

It is firmly established by decades of research that the ability to read text fluently is an essential factor in skillful reading (NRP, 2000). Primary school teachers assess their pupils' fluency, often several times a year, and include lessons to build pupils' fluency. We know reading fluency is important.

Defining fluency

There are several misunderstandings about reading fluency, the primary one being that reading fluently means reading fast. While "speed" (rate) is definitely one component of reading fluency, it is not the key component, and there are other important factors for educators to consider when teaching and assessing fluency.

Hasbrouck and Glaser (2019) define passage reading fluency as the ability to read text

- with reasonable accuracy
- at an appropriate rate
- with suitable expression
- that leads to accurate and deep comprehension and motivation to read

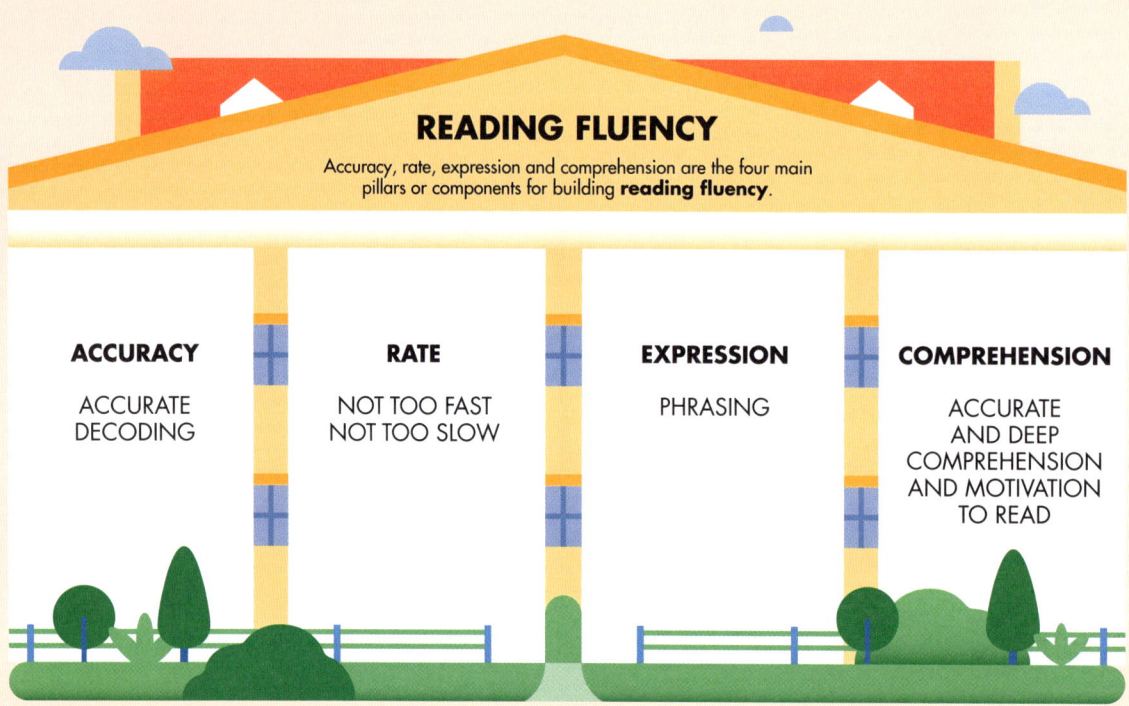

Average passage reading WCPM, by NAEP reading achievement level and below NAEP Basic subgroup: 2018 (White et al. 2021)

The study by White et al. (2021) examined the average passage reading fluency, measured in words correct per minute (WCPM), among 4th-grade pupils in relation to their NAEP reading achievement levels.

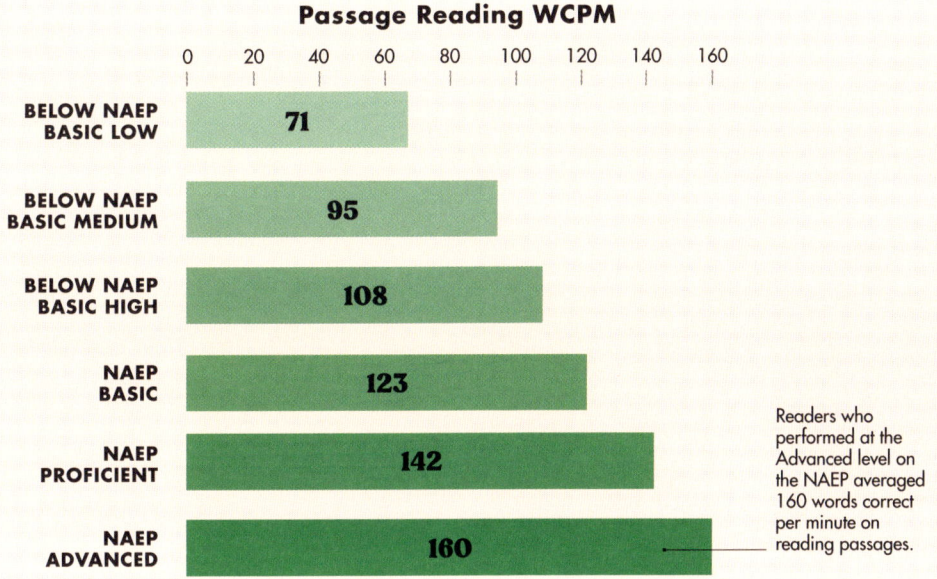

Readers who performed at the Advanced level on the NAEP averaged 160 words correct per minute on reading passages.

Accuracy: We list accuracy first in our definition to make the point that – if comprehension of text is the goal of reading – then accuracy must be first, foremost and forever the key aspect of fluency because a reader needs to be able to read text at a minimum of 95% accuracy (correctly identifying the words and their meanings) to be able to understand what they read. Reasonable accuracy is the foundation of reading fluency if comprehension is the goal.

Rate: A 2018 study by White et al. determined that various levels of automaticity predicted pupils' performance on the 4th grade National Assessment of Educational Progress (NAEP) from Advanced to Proficient to Basic and Below Basic. Their findings aligned with the 2017 ORF norms compiled by Hasbrouck & Tindal. In this study the readers who performed at the Advanced level on the NAEP read on average 160 WCPM, which is the 75th percentile on the 2017 spring 4th grade norms in the Hasbrouck and Tindal study. The Proficient to Basic readers ranged from 142 to 123 WCPM, which is a range of approximately 10 words plus and minus around the Hasbrouck and Tindal 50th percentile (133 WCPM). Those pupils who performed at the Below Basic level were reading at around the 25th percentile or lower.

These results show that rate (assessed as words correct per minute) makes a difference in reading outcomes, but that reading "faster" is not the goal. The White et al. study and others seem to suggest that a rate at the 75th percentile appears sufficient for optimising comprehension while the 50th percentile is necessary for grade-level comprehension of text. Reading either too quickly for the brain to process the information or reading too slowly impedes comprehension.

Expression: Reading with expression (the pitch, tone, volume, emphasis, rhythm and phrasing of reading) is another component of text reading fluency. Reading expression is sometimes referred to as "prosody". However, while accuracy and rate both clearly contribute to a reader's ability to comprehend the text they are reading, researchers often discuss expression as an outcome of comprehension. While knowing how to interpret punctuation and diacritical marks in text such as full stops, commas, question marks and accent marks help a reader make text sound like speech (Stahl & Kuhn, 2002) and therefore easier to comprehend, the ability to read with accurate expression is best seen as an outcome of comprehending the text being read (Groen et al., 2019).

Assessing fluency

If we think about passage reading fluency as the ability to read text with reasonable accuracy, appropriate rate, with suitable expression, then an assessment of a pupil's ability to read fluently would need to assess each of these components. This can be achieved by having a pupil read aloud from a piece of unpractised text and calculating an overall score of accuracy (the percent of words read correctly), rate (the number of words read correctly per minute) and an observation and rating of expression, perhaps using a rating scale such as one created by Zutell and Rasinski (1991). Educators should also do a check of the pupil's understanding of the text when they have finished reading.

If a pupil is unable to read a passage at their current grade level with reasonable accuracy (at least 95% correct), with appropriate rate near or above the 50th percentile on the Hasbrouck and Tindal (2017) norms, with suitable expression, and particularly if they have difficulty understanding the text, additional assessments should be administered to determine why they are struggling to read fluently at grade level. Having them attempt to read text at lower reading levels should be considered, along with assessments of phonics, decoding and vocabulary as appropriate.

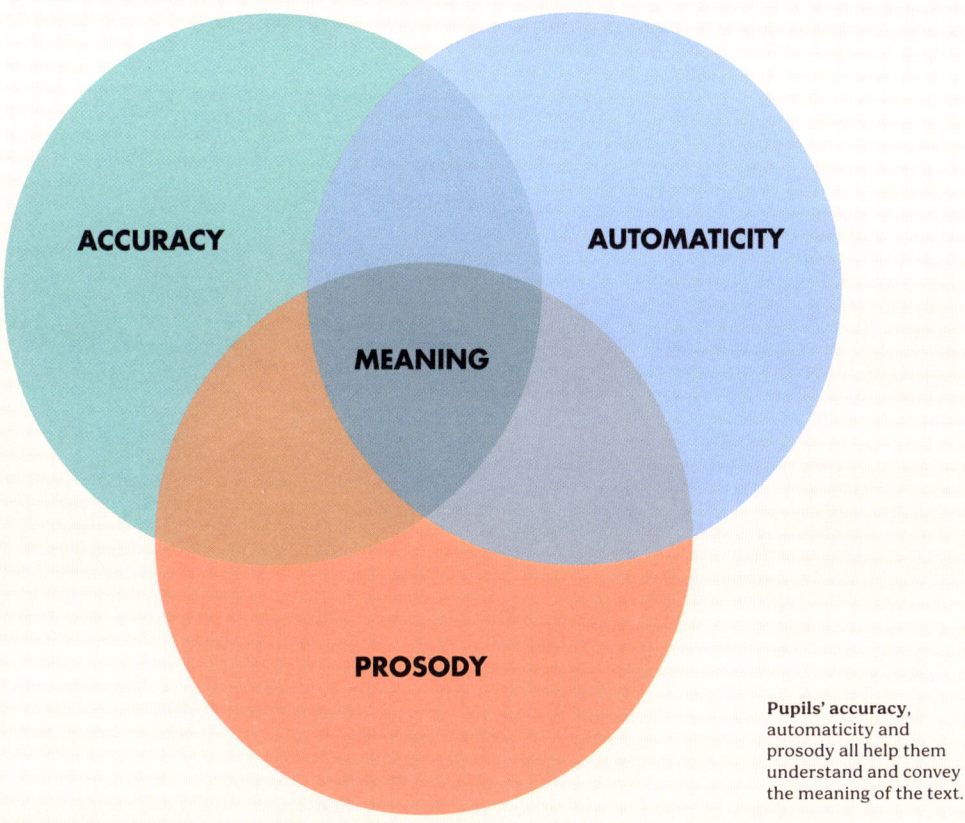

Pupils' accuracy, automaticity and prosody all help them understand and convey the meaning of the text.

Teaching fluency

We want all pupils to read age-appropriate texts with fluency and understanding. Achieving this requires attending to fluency at the earliest stages of reading. Wolf and Katzir-Cohen (2001) remind us that fluency develops in progressions. We teach pupils to be accurate and then automatic in identifying letter names and sounds. This emphasis on accuracy followed by automaticity continues as pupils learn to read words, phrases and meaningful text.

Hasbrouck and Glaser (2019) suggest using a framework of fluency instruction called Triple A:

- **A: Accuracy**
- **A: Automaticity**
- **A: Access meaning**

Teach pupils to accurately identify and understand the meaning and purpose of words (accuracy).

Demonstrate how to read words, phrases and text with appropriate rate and expression, providing ample practice to achieve fluency (automaticity).

From the start, teach that reading has a purpose: comprehending what is read. Keep pupils accountable for considering meaning throughout the lesson (access meaning).

Conclusion

Reading fluency plays a key role in our pupils' success. It's important to understand fluency, how to assess it and how to teach it effectively. Remember, fluent reading isn't about reading fast!

Research-Backed Ways to Teach Vocabulary

by Melissa Loftus and Lori Sappington

Vocabulary makes or breaks pupils' comprehension. Research shows how to teach vocabulary by connecting words to real-world experiences and concepts.

To truly understand what we read, we must be able to process the meaning of the words. Pupils learn words in two ways: through direct instruction of important words and by using strategies to figure out new words.

Some vocabulary words need to be taught directly, with clear definitions, examples and practice. When teaching words explicitly, focus on useful words that help pupils understand a text, or are likely to appear in other texts.

On the other hand, word-learning strategies like breaking down word parts (morphology), exploring word origins (etymology) and using context clues help pupils learn new words on their own. Give pupils opportunities to explore words through rich texts and engaging language experiences.

When teaching vocabulary, keep in mind these five research-based principles: **meanings, connection, usage, repetition** and **collaboration** (Loftus & Sappington, 2024, p. 120).

Semantic mapping
This process helps pupils understand how words are linked.

Meanings and connections

To build long-lasting word knowledge, pupils need to fully understand what a word means— not just memorise a dictionary definition! To help pupils truly grasp the meaning of words, encourage them to draw pictures, act out definitions and provide examples.

Pupils also need to see how words and concepts are related to each other. One fun way to do this is through something called **semantic mapping**. This helps pupils see how new words are linked to other words and ideas. For example, think about the phrase "outer space".

What other words or phrases come to mind? You might think of *stars, astronauts, galaxies, planets, constellations* or *the solar system*.

A **vocabulary continuum** is a great way to explore shades of meaning among words. For example, pupils might think about words like *infinite, spacious, immense, large* and *enormous*. They can place the words on a continuum to show how their meanings are related but slightly different.

Vocabulary continuum

LARGE — SPACIOUS — ENORMOUS — IMMENSE — INFINITE

A vocabulary continuum shows subtle differences in meaning between similar words.

Semantic map

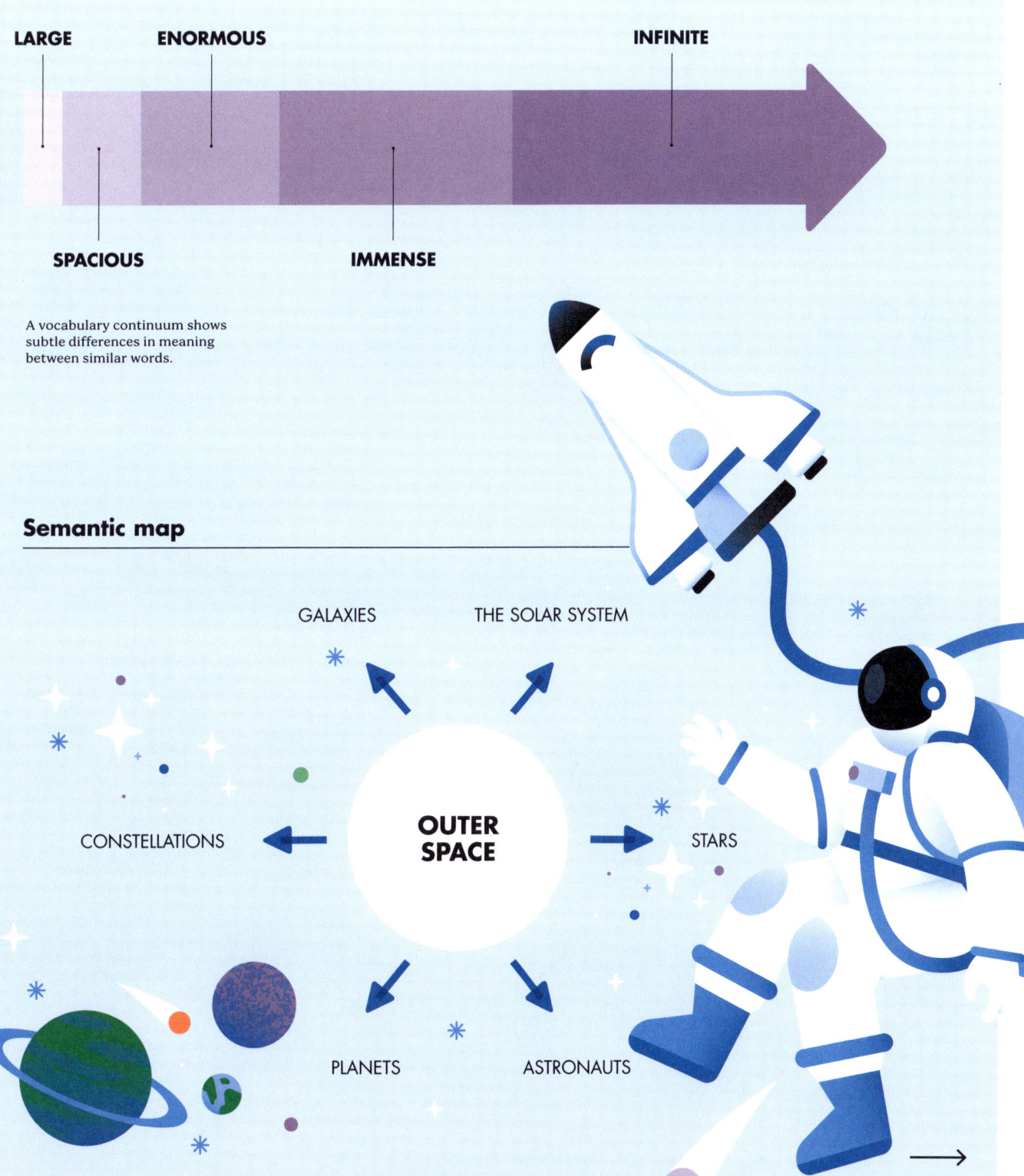

OUTER SPACE
- GALAXIES
- THE SOLAR SYSTEM
- STARS
- ASTRONAUTS
- PLANETS
- CONSTELLATIONS

> **"To help pupils remember words, encourage them to use and repeat them often. The more they say a word, the easier it is to remember its meaning."**

Usage and repetition

To help pupils remember words, encourage them to use and repeat them often. The more they say a word, the easier it is to remember its meaning. Encourage them to use new words before, during and after reading–in both speaking and writing. Also, teach vocabulary in a cycle. Revisit words you've already taught to help pupils make connections over time.

Collaboration

Create a classroom where pupils pay attention to the words they already know—and the ones they don't. Teach some words directly, and show pupils helpful ways to learn new words on their own.

Let's look at how vocabulary instruction for the word *gravity* might unfold in a science lesson about outer space.

- **Say the word:** Say *gravity* clearly and slowly, then have pupils repeat it to practise pronunciation.
- **Explain the meaning:** Explain that *gravity* is a force that pulls objects toward each other. For example, gravity pulls everything toward Earth, which is why we don't float away.
- **Make it real:** Demonstrate *gravity* by dropping an object and having pupils observe how it falls.
- **Practise using the word:** Have pupils use *gravity* in writing and discussions, exploring how it affects objects on Earth and in space.
- **Encourage ongoing use:** Keep *gravity* in ongoing discussions. Have pupils write short descriptions or create diagrams showing how gravity works, reinforcing the concept over time.

These steps not only build pupils' vocabulary but also help them connect the word *gravity* to real-world experiences and scientific concepts, deepening their understanding.

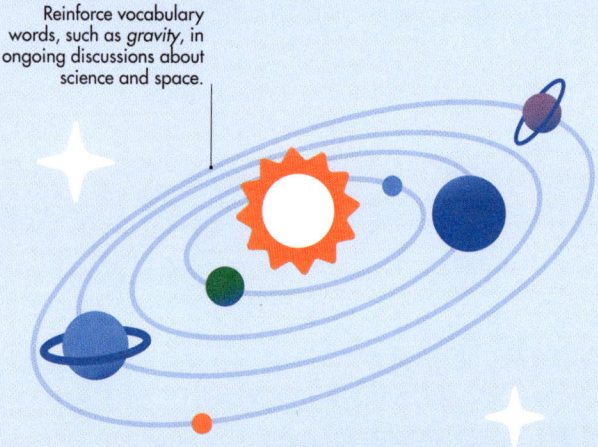

Reinforce vocabulary words, such as *gravity*, in ongoing discussions about science and space.

Independent Reading

by Patricia Bryant

Fostering a true love for reading goes beyond teaching techniques. It's about inspiring an internal drive that makes reading a cherished activity.

During the early stages of developing basic reading skills, it's natural to encourage a child to practise reading independently. However, recent studies reveal a continuous decline in children reading for enjoyment. While the exact causes remain unclear, factors such as the prevalence of technology and the rise of social media are often cited as potential contributors. Interestingly, children who do find joy in reading tend to perform better on standardised tests compared to their peers who are less inclined to read. So what can we do to improve this?

Independent reading extends beyond mastering foundational reading skills. It involves more than assessing whether a child can independently apply taught strategies; it marks the beginning of a lifelong relationship with reading. Will they embrace reading as a cherished hobby or will it become a chore they seek to avoid? That's not something that you can teach, but something you can encourage.

"Recent studies reveal a continuous decline in children reading for enjoyment."

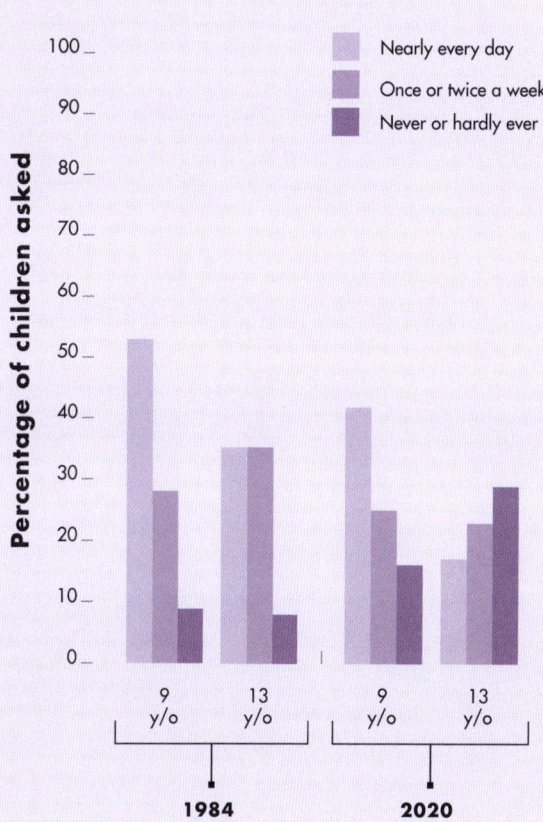

The numbers of children reading for pleasure have decreased over time, based on surveys of US pupils (US Department of Education).

Even as adults, we sometimes develop aversions to certain hobbies or interests due to negative experiences. These associations, when reinforced, can deter us from engaging further. For children, this formative period is an opportunity to focus less on demonstrating reading skills and more on fostering a genuine love for books. The following strategies can help cultivate independent reading among children.

Let them choose their books

Allowing children to select their own books – guided by teachers, librarians, or parents – encourages exploration and sparks interest. When a child reads a book they enjoy, it can ignite a passion for specific genres. Even if they dislike a book, it's a valuable learning experience, helping them discover their preferences.

Recommend books based on their interests

Tailored recommendations can deepen engagement and build trust. For example, I once recommended the Cirque du Freak series to a 5th-grade pupil interested in vampires. They became so captivated that they read the series from start to finish. Similarly, suggesting Nancy Drew to a pupil who loved strong heroines encouraged her to explore other genres, even if that particular series didn't resonate.

Introduce chapter books gradually

Younger children are naturally drawn to picture books, making them an excellent gateway to chapter books with illustrations. These transitional books can help children eventually use their imagination to engage with text-heavy novels.

Encourage exploration of challenging books

Letting children attempt more advanced books can foster pride and ownership in their reading journey. For instance, my seven-year-old niece once picked up a large book on Impressionist art. Enthralled by the vibrant images, she attempted to decode terms like *abstract* and even ventured into French words like *nouveau* and *avant-garde*. While she didn't grasp all the concepts, the experience left her with a sense of accomplishment and curiosity.

Expand their horizons

Expose children to a variety of genres. Fiction can branch into historical or science fiction, while nonfiction can include biographies, science facts or culturally relevant topics. Expanding their options broadens their understanding of the world and deepens their interests.

Explore non-traditional reading formats

Reading isn't limited to traditional books. Encourage children to engage with graphic novels, recipe books, craft guides or other formats. These alternatives can connect reading with hands-on activities, sparking diverse interests and enriching their experiences.

Expanding horizons
Exploring new genres or formats can deepen children's understanding.

Create comfortable reading spaces

Just as adults enjoy reading in cozy, quiet settings, children also benefit from inviting spaces that make reading enjoyable. Consider setting up a reading corner with a comfy chair or beanbag. For added fun, try themed activities like "Teatime Reading Fridays", where children can read while sipping tea or hot chocolate and engage in discussions with peers or adults. These special moments can make reading feel more like a cherished activity than a task.

By adopting these strategies, we can nurture a lifelong love for reading in children, allowing them to view books as sources of joy, inspiration and growth rather than obligation. After all, inspiring a devotion to reading isn't just about teaching techniques. It's about sparking an internal drive, which isn't always something that can be taught.

> "Younger children are naturally drawn to picture books, making them an excellent gateway to chapter books with illustrations."

Developing Deep Understanding Through Close Reading

by Keshiea Chandler

Close reading empowers pupils to dive beneath the surface of texts, using specific strategies to uncover deeper meaning and build critical thinking skills that enhance overall reading comprehension.

Close reading is like being a reading detective. It's a careful, purposeful way of reading that helps us understand texts at a deeper level. Instead of simply rushing through a passage to get the main idea, close reading involves examining the text multiple times, each time with a different focus. This approach helps readers notice important details, understand the author's choices and make meaningful connections.

The three-read method

An effective close reading typically involves reading a text at least three times, with each read serving a different purpose. The initial reading focuses on understanding the basic content, where readers explore what the text is mainly about, who the key characters are or what main ideas are being presented. This first encounter with the text builds a crucial foundation for deeper analysis.

The second reading takes readers deeper as they examine how the text is constructed. During this stage, readers pay special attention to the author's craft on how specific word choices impact meaning and tone, how the organisation of ideas shapes understanding, and how literary devices or text features enhance the overall message. Readers might notice

FIRST READ — Understanding the content

SECOND READ — Analysing features and author's craft

THIRD READ — Making connections

how a metaphor illuminates a complex concept or how the pacing of sentences creates emotional impact.

The third and final reading connects the text to broader ideas and personal experiences. At this stage, readers reflect on how the text resonates with their own lives, discovering connections to other texts they've read or knowledge they possess. They consider the broader implications of the message and often find themselves pondering questions that remain unanswered, which is a sign of genuine engagement with the material.

Making close reading accessible

For both young readers and those new to close reading, visual supports can make the process more manageable and engaging. Teachers often encourage pupils to use different coloured highlighters for each reading focus, creating a visual representation of their thinking journey through the text. Some classrooms develop special annotation symbols that pupils use to mark different types of observations, while others find success in breaking longer texts into smaller, more digestible chunks. Sticky notes serve as valuable tools for tracking thinking, allowing readers to document their observations and questions without marking the text directly.

The impact on reading development

When readers engage in close reading regularly, they develop a sophisticated set of skills that naturally transfer to their everyday reading experiences. Critical thinking and analysis become second nature as readers learn to examine texts more carefully. Their attention to detail sharpens, and they become more adept at supporting their ideas with evidence from the text. Perhaps most

> **"Close reading is like being a reading detective; it's a careful, purposeful way of reading that helps us understand texts at a deeper level."**

importantly, readers develop deep comprehension skills and independent reading strategies that serve them well across all subject areas.

Supporting close reading at home

Parents and caregivers play a vital role in nurturing close reading skills outside the classroom. They can model careful reading by sharing interesting texts and thinking aloud about their own reading process. When discussing books or articles with children, parents can ask questions that prompt deeper thinking and encourage rereading when the meaning isn't clear. Family discussions about authors' choices and their effects can help young readers understand how writers craft their messages. Most importantly, celebrating the discoveries made during close reading helps create a positive association with this deeper approach to understanding texts.

Through regular practice and support, close reading becomes not just a classroom strategy but a valuable life skill that enhances understanding and appreciation of all types of texts.

Interrupted Reading

by Jennifer D. Morrison

This article explores interrupted reading, a technique designed to help pupils navigate complex texts. This method empowers learners to engage deeply with their reading material.

An interrupted reading is a close reading structure used to support pupils in reading more difficult pieces of text (Shea et al., 2013). It is an investigation of a short piece of text and is one of the multiple readings of this chosen texts within an instructional sequence (Brown & Kappes, 2012). It uses text-based questions and discussion to guide pupils to deeply analyse and appreciate various aspects of the text. It is particularly effective for older pupils, including adolescents and adults, who are learning to unpack more complex, abstract and disciplinary-specific texts. Through the use of chunking and delayed advancement into the text, pupils are better able to process the text and more closely examine aspects such as diction, author's craft, syntax, symbolism, form and tone. It guides pupils' deconstruction and then reconstruction of text to make deeper, richer meaning of it (Morrison, 2020). It engages pupils in critical thinking and critical reading that empower individuals to be transformed by their text interactions and avoid "uncritically conform[ing] in many domains of our personal lives" (Paul & Elder, 2005, p. 22). An interrupted reading can serve as a rich prelude to pupils' engaging in subsequent discourse, written analysis or emulated writing based on the text and their responses to it.

Chunking
A reading strategy that involves breaking a text into smaller, manageable segments or "chunks".

Benefits of interrupted reading

The reading is "interrupted" because readers see only one portion – or chunk – of the text at a time. For younger readers, the chunked text helps them better decode and make meaning without being overwhelmed with large amounts of written words on the screen or page. For older pupils, it can slow them down; help them examine the text in a more focused, intense manner; encourage greater personal connection with the text and support them in learning to unpack ever more complex and disciplinary-specific texts (Morrison, 2020).

Selecting and chunking the text

In order to conduct an interrupted reading, you must first select a rich, deep, multifaceted text. This may be a short article, a poem or a poignant section of a book. It may be nonfiction or fiction text, a speech, a news article, an opinion piece or another complex text that requires a close, thoughtful read. Then identify natural breaks in the text and create chunks. Morrison (2020) discusses how she used the introduction to Martin Luther King Jr.'s book *Why We Can't Wait* (1964) as an interrupted reading with 11th grade AP Language pupils. The approximately 800-word introduction was strategically broken into an 11-page booklet with anywhere from a single sentence to a paragraph printed in an enlarged font on each page.

Conducting an interrupted reading

To conduct the interrupted reading, pupils are handed the packet face down and asked to either have pen and paper or a laptop ready for them to respond. They should create a heading for each page (page 1, page 2) in order to delineate which notes go with which page of the interrupted reading. Pupils are instructed that they may write down anything they notice, think about or consider as they read the text chunk. They are not allowed to move forward in the packet until the teacher tells them to do so. They may, however, choose to go back, revisit a previous page and add notes as they advance into the text.

Encouraging open responses

When told to begin, pupils flip the packet over and read the initial chunk of text. They then record their thoughts and observations on paper or in a Word document. For example, in Morrison's (2020) example, the first page consists of the single first sentence of MLK's essay: "It is the beginning of the year of our Lord 1963." Pupils may know in 1963 the Civil Rights movement was occurring in the US. They may note that the "beginning of the year" could refer to January or winter. It is important to allow pupils to respond openly. This allows them to think creatively and be open to meaning-making and interpretation.

Guiding discussion after interrupted reading

Once pupils have responded to the text on the first page, the teacher asks them to turn to the next page, where again they read, mark the text and respond in their ongoing notes. This process continues until pupils have responded to each page (chunk) of the chosen text. At the end, the teacher encourages them to go back to earlier pages and add to their notes.

Once the interrupted reading process is completed, the teacher can lead a conversation about what pupils responded to. Morrison (2020) describes how she listed each page of the interrupted reading on whiteboards around the classroom and had pupils offer their responses. The teacher should have designed key questions regarding the text to frame the ensuing discussion.

Once this deconstructive process is completed, it is important to have pupils synthesise their learning and reconstruct the text. This can be done by having pupils write an analysis, illustrate a key idea, make thematic connections with other texts or use other ways of having pupils express their learning.

Interrupted reading helps pupils process information more effectively without feeling overwhelmed. By focusing on one chunk at a time, learners can concentrate on understanding the content, analysing its structure and recognising key concepts.

Sharing Text with Paired Oral Reading

by Jake Downs

Shared reading experiences provide a powerful, effective way for parents and teachers to support young readers' fluency and comprehension.

Reading text with a pupil is a time-honoured approach to promoting reading proficiency. Even so, some teachers and parents may wonder how to make their reading time as productive as possible. One practical approach to making shared reading more beneficial is Synchronous Paired Oral Reading Techniques (SPORT; Downs & Mohr, 2024). With over 60 years of research, the evidence indicates that SPORT can promote oral reading fluency and comprehension development for young readers (Downs et al., 2023).

The approach of SPORT is simple – a tutor and tutee read connected text synchronously (or at the same time) out loud. The tutor can be a more proficient same-age or older peer, but is often an adult. Beyond this basic framework, keep in mind these key considerations for SPORT when you adopt the SPORT approach.

Age and proficiency

The only prerequisite of SPORT is that the reader has enough decoding skill to read connected text. Beyond that, SPORT is likely beneficial to pupils across a range of ages and reading proficiencies. Pupils needing accelerated growth in accuracy, fluency or comprehension when reading might be particularly good candidates.

Frequency and length

Session frequency and length can be adapted to the reader, but research suggests 15–20 minutes a few times a week will promote fluency and comprehension growth (Downs & Mohr, 2024).

Text and difficulty level

Synchronous choral reading is a robust scaffold for the pupil. Hence, research has found that pupils in SPORT can access – and benefit from – texts above their independent reading level. In multiple studies, pupils participating in same-age SPORT have outperformed a control group in text two or more year groups above their independent reading level (Brown et al., 2018; Downs et al., 2020). These data indicate that with tutor support, pupils can tackle texts significantly more difficult than what they could read on their own.

Effectively, with SPORT, challenging text becomes a catalyst rather than a barrier. As a result, a text's difficulty level should be a secondary consideration when selecting reading materials. Instead, prioritise pupil interest and the relevance of the text content when designing a SPORT plan.

Pupil interest

What books is your pupil interested in reading? Use this opportunity to explore texts that your pupil would not – or could not – access independently. A good place to start is to ask your pupil what texts they would be interested in reading. However, you may need to try other approaches if your pupil doesn't know or have a strong opinion of preferred texts. One approach uses a genre wheel, where each section represents a different genre or style of text while also allowing for pupil choice (Reutzel et al., 2008). Alternatively, curate 5–7 interesting texts and allow the pupil to select from this set (Morgan et al., 2000; Downs et al., 2020).

Content areas

SPORT can also be used to build knowledge in age-appropriate content areas such as science or social studies. In this approach, you can curate a set of related texts on a specific topic. Each of these texts could be shorter – perhaps one text per session – but over the course of several weeks, regular SPORT sessions could help build important knowledge in the desired area. For instance, if a primary school pupil is beginning a science unit on ecosystems in November, the SPORT dyad could spend October reading texts that demonstrate how energy moves through an ecosystem.

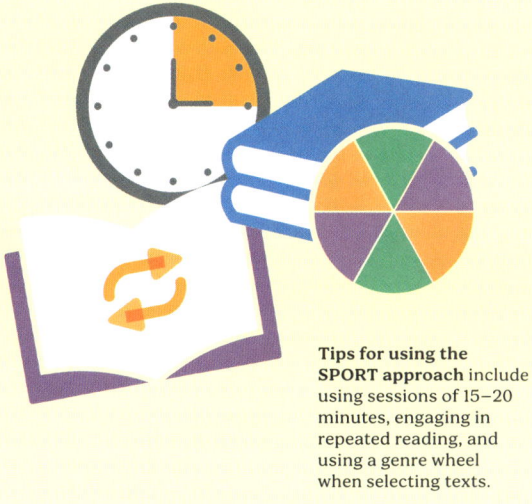

Tips for using the SPORT approach include using sessions of 15–20 minutes, engaging in repeated reading, and using a genre wheel when selecting texts.

Paired oral reading
Parents and teachers can read with pupils to support fluency and comprehension.

Adaptations

The basic structure of SPORT is simple – the tutor and pupil chorally read connected text. However, SPORT is flexible and amenable to adaptation. Depending on the pupil's needs, you may wish to incorporate the following adaptations to more robustly support your pupil.

Repeated reading

Several studies have investigated incorporating repeated reading into the basic SPORT structure (Young et al., 2018; Young et al., 2020). When incorporating repeated reading, the tutor will periodically pause and ask the pupil to reread a section of text. Initially—and depending on the pupil—you could ask the pupil to reread a sentence or paragraph, but then over sessions gradually progress to a half or whole page of rereading. Incorporating repeated reading will primarily support your pupil's automaticity, but will also likely benefit comprehension as well.

> **"Shared reading is also beneficial for pupils who are not yet reading or just beginning to read."**

Multisyllabic support

Pupils are often challenged by reading long words—yet often these words carry significant meaning in the text. If you want to support your pupil in reading the complex words, briefly preview the text and select 3–5 words to write on a paper or a small white board (cf., Downs et al., manuscript in preparation). Then, model for your pupil how to blend these words using a flexible strategy and allow brief practice before beginning the text.

Summarising

Summarising text at the end of the session – orally or in a written format – is an excellent approach to support text comprehension (Filderman et al., 2022). This wrap-up could take the form of a gist – also known as a ten-word takeaway – which summarises the reading in a single sentence (Vaughn et al., 2022). A full summary containing key ideas and supporting details is also effective. You may wish to model this process for your pupil and provide interactive support to develop an accurate summary.

Early readers

Shared reading is also beneficial for pupils who are not yet reading, or just beginning to read. Select an engaging text to read aloud to your pupil. Then, as you read, call your pupil's attention to various features of print such as the author, the book title, headings and captions (Piasta et al., 2012). Also, show your pupil that print is read from left to right and top to bottom. If your pupil has some basic alphabet knowledge, you can point to a letter and ask the pupil to say the letter name and letter sound or ask pupils to decode some of the basic words in the text (Justice et al., 2009). Last, use serve-and-return dialogue, such as the Strive for Five approach (Cabell & Zucker, 2024), to promote rich language development with your pupil.

Conclusion

SPORT is an evidence-based approach that parents and teachers can use to promote the reading fluency and comprehension of young readers. One major advantage of SPORT is that it is easy to implement, flexible and inexpensive. However, SPORT is likely best leveraged when deployed alongside other evidence based practices in word reading, fluency and comprehension. Ultimately, careful consideration of your pupil and their reading needs can productively inform how you use SPORT.

"**Reading engagement is central to both the Science of Reading and best practices in reading instruction.**"

Evan Ortlieb

Reading Motivation

by Seth A. Parsons

Teachers and specialists can supercharge their instruction by not only teaching the strategies pupils need to read but also attending to pupils' motivation.

Teachers, especially primary school teachers, have recently heard a lot about "the science of reading". This phrase is being used so frequently to support so many recommendations and instructional changes that it is difficult to nail down what, exactly, it means. It seems to me that we currently have "the science of reading" and "The Science of Reading". The science of reading is easy to define: it is the scientific research base on how people learn to read. The Science of Reading is much more difficult to define because it is a movement, an initiative that individuals are advocating as evidenced by The Science of Reading legislation now in 40 states plus the District of Columbia.

I'm a literacy scholar who studies reading motivation, and I can tell you unequivocally that the science of reading includes much insight into reading motivation and how to enhance pupils' motivation to read (Erickson, 2019; Erickson & Wharton-McDonald, 2019; Schiefele et al., 2012; Stutz et al., 2016; Toste et al., 2020). Curiously, though, The Science of Reading movement pays little, if any, attention to reading motivation (Parsons & Erickson, 2024). Nonetheless, in the following I provide an overview of what the research base *does* say about how to support pupils' motivation to read.

The research on reading motivation

Logically, it makes sense that we would want pupils to be motivated readers. However, a robust collection of research has also established that reading motivation is strongly associated with reading achievement (Schiefele et al., 2012; Stutz et al., 2016; Toste et al., 2020). For example, Scheifele and colleagues (2016) investigated the relationship between reading motivation and reading comprehension with early primary school pupils. They concluded that "the findings suggest that even at early stages of learning to read, intrinsic reading motivation contributes to pupils' development of reading competence" (p. 49). Research has also demonstrated aspects of literacy instruction that are particularly motivating. Self-Determination Theory demonstrates that when pupils' psychological needs of competence, relatedness and autonomy are met, they are more likely to be motivated (Ryan & Deci, 2017). This understanding provides insight into aspects of literacy instruction that are motivating, including (a) appropriate challenge, (b) collaboration, (c) high-interest texts and (d) pupil choice (Guthrie & Humenick, 2004; Erickson, 2019; Miller & Meece, 1999; Parsons & Erickson, 2024; Turner, 1995).

> **Self-determination theory**
> Suggests that pupils are motivated when certain psychological needs are met.

Challenge and collaboration

Pupils are optimally motivated to read when their work is appropriately challenging. Work that is too difficult leads to frustration and can lead to poor self-concept as a reader, which is demotivating. Conversely, pupils are easily bored by work that is too easy. This focus on appropriate challenge aligns with learning as well. Vygotsky (1978) presented the Zone of Proximal Development, just beyond what pupils can do independently, as the place where pupils learn best. Appropriate challenge supports pupils' feelings of competence because it allows them to operate within their zone of proximal development.

Providing pupils opportunities to collaborate in their literacy work is likely to support pupil motivation to read (Guthrie & Humenick, 2004). Reading is a social activity, and children are social beings (Vygotsky, 1978). Turner (1995) found that collaboration was an important factor in pupils' reading motivation. Collaborating with peers to accomplish shared goals supports feelings of belongingness, further supporting pupils' motivation (Ryan & Deci, 2017). Peer collaboration supports not only pupils' motivation but also their literacy learning (Murphy et al., 2009).

Pupil choice

The last two components of literacy instruction that are supportive for motivation are high-interest material and pupil choice (Guthrie & Humenick, 2004). Just like you and me, pupils prefer to read texts and explore topics that are interesting to them. For this reason, it is important for teachers to get to know their pupils well. This allows teachers to align content with pupils' interests. Similarly, when pupils have choice, they are more invested in the work (Ives et al., 2021).

Pupil reading motivation is heightened by appropriate challenge, collaboration, high-interest material and choice (Guthrie & Humenick, 2004; Erickson, 2019; Miller & Meece, 1999; Parsons & Erickson, 2024; Turner, 1995). An exciting note here is that all these motivating features of literacy instruction can easily be infused into The Science of Reading curricula.

> "Work that is too difficult leads to frustration and can lead to poor self-concept as a reader."

Zone of proximal development

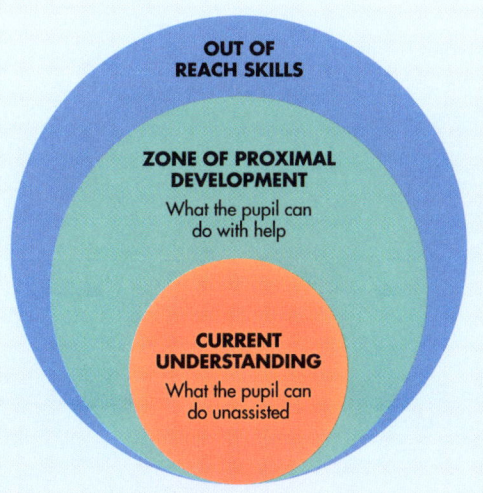

Lev Vygotsky theorised that pupils learn best at the Zone of Proximal Development, just beyond what they can do independently.

Reading Engagement

by Evan Ortlieb

Reading engagement goes beyond simply reading text – it involves emotional, cognitive and behavioural connections that enhance comprehension. This article explores strategies for fostering engaged readers and cultivating meaningful literacy experiences in classrooms.

Reading engagement is defined as the level of interest, motivation and involvement with a text. It is more than just the act of reading. It involves the emotional and cognitive connections a reader makes during and after reading. These connections relate to a reader's interaction with the material, others and overall sense making (Aukerman & Chambers Schuldt, 2021). High levels of reading engagement are correlated with improved comprehension (Duke, Ward, & Pearson, 2021) and school retention rates (Reschly, 2009).

The impact of reading engagement on learning

Reading engagement is foundational to both the planning of literacy instruction and the physical act of reading itself. Ultimately, it determines the degree to which content is learned and reading habits are developed. Cultivating learning environments that engage readers is the focus of this article, as everyone (including the most resistant readers) is capable of being engaged in reading activities.

Creating engaging literacy environments

Optimising instruction requires a specific focus on engaging readers in and beyond the curriculum. Making reading a group activity is the most important aspect to engage learners. Conversely, the more that reading occurs in solitude and without peer engagement, the less likely it is to become a habit or preferred activity. The importance of positioning groups of pupils to question, discuss, predict, critique, consider and connect with what they read cannot be overstated. These social reading environments are natural extensions of human development and desires to interact with each other, particularly for those with special educational needs (Ambarchi et al., 2024).

Strategies for sustaining pupil engagement

How can teachers prepare lessons that position their learners to be fully engaged and sustain engagement? A variety of cognitive, behavioural and emotional considerations should guide their considerations, as these elements comprise the three dimensions of reading engagement.

Cognitive factors

Reading experiences must attract learners to the subject matter and/or method of presenting the content. People are intrigued by scary stories, science experiments, incredible feats, thriller movies, sports competitions and new discoveries because they captivate the learner with novel experiences.

Attraction theory (Ortlieb, 2014) suggests that a multi-step process can facilitate improved rates of readers attending to literary experiences. Beginning a lesson with a jolt to learners' existing knowledge or experiential base can cause mental perturbation, driving them to

ADVANCED READING SKILLS AND STRATEGIES 79

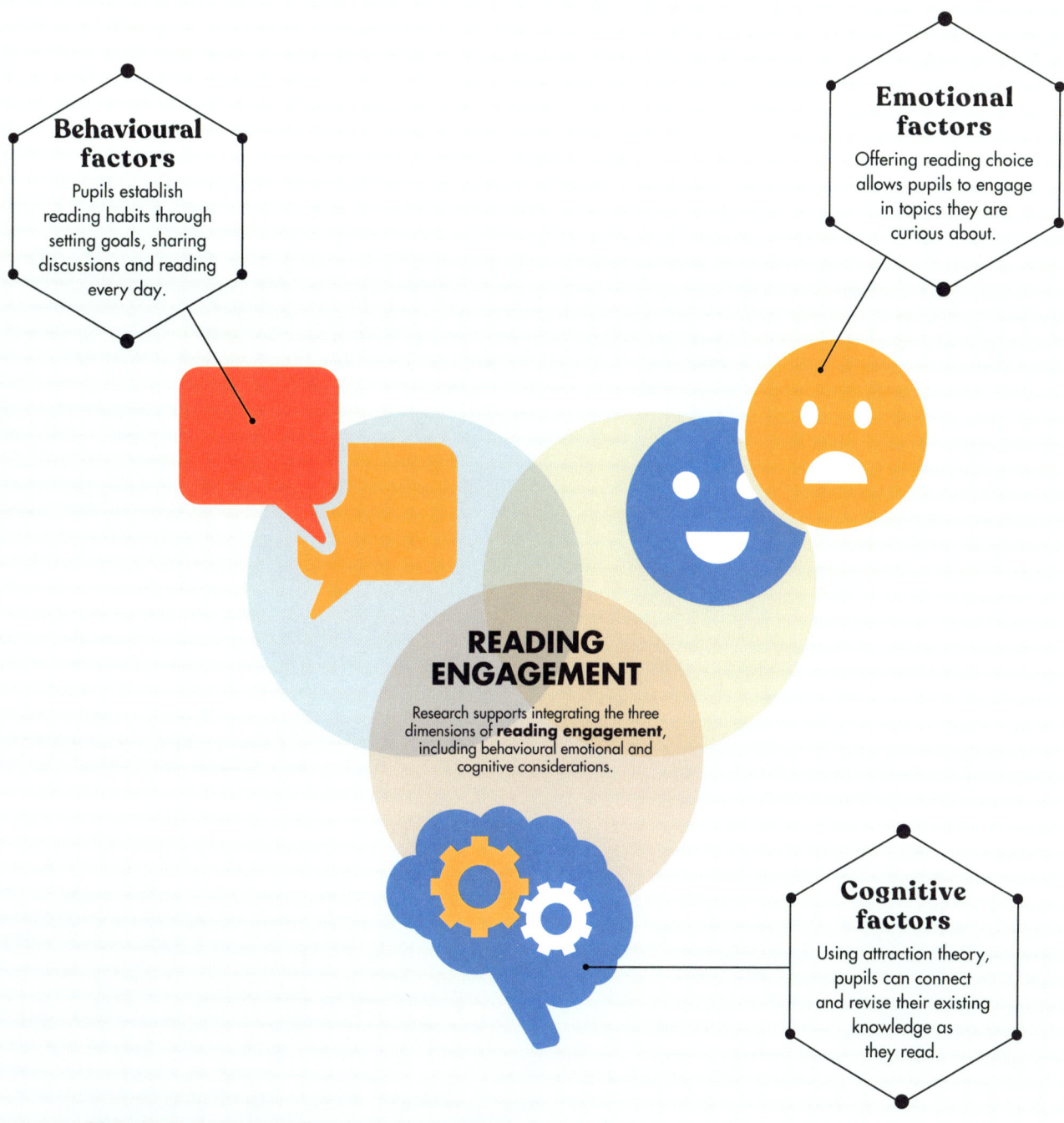

Behavioural factors
Pupils establish reading habits through setting goals, sharing discussions and reading every day.

Emotional factors
Offering reading choice allows pupils to engage in topics they are curious about.

READING ENGAGEMENT
Research supports integrating the three dimensions of **reading engagement**, including behavioural emotional and cognitive considerations.

Cognitive factors
Using attraction theory, pupils can connect and revise their existing knowledge as they read.

"High levels of reading engagement are correlated with improved comprehension and school retention rates."

become roused, piquing their curiosity and questioning its basis. For example, a primary school teacher might discuss how fish are cold-blooded vertebrates. Beginning this lesson with the novel aspect that some fish can walk on land (e.g. mudskippers) may cause learners to question their existing way of understanding what a fish is, also known as cognitive dissonance. This stretches learners' cognition, causing them to engage with content in novel ways. These new approaches add to their overall understanding through literary activities that can include discussion, videos, tutorials and text-based investigations used to determine content-based takeaways from the lesson.

The components of attraction theory work in unison to prompt pupils to take an initial stimulus and progress through critical thinking processes leading up to knowledge acquisition, organisation and synthesis. Becoming active learners is necessary for pupils to regain interest in furthering their education, personal literacies and career opportunities.

Decreasing the number of distractions and minimising multi-tasking support one's metacognition of a single task. Strategies such as think-alouds and questioning support pupils' active engagement while reading; however, these strategies must be explicitly taught in context and modelled regularly as approaches that effective readers use to monitor their understanding while reading. The use of graphic organisers can also aid reading comprehension, granted not everyone will align with every reading task. The contemplation and careful selection of which graphic organisers to use and when to use them are learned over time and with practice.

Behavioural factors

Reading habits are developed in reading-rich environments where time is allocated to daily reading. Emphasising reading to explore curiosities through selecting texts of choice

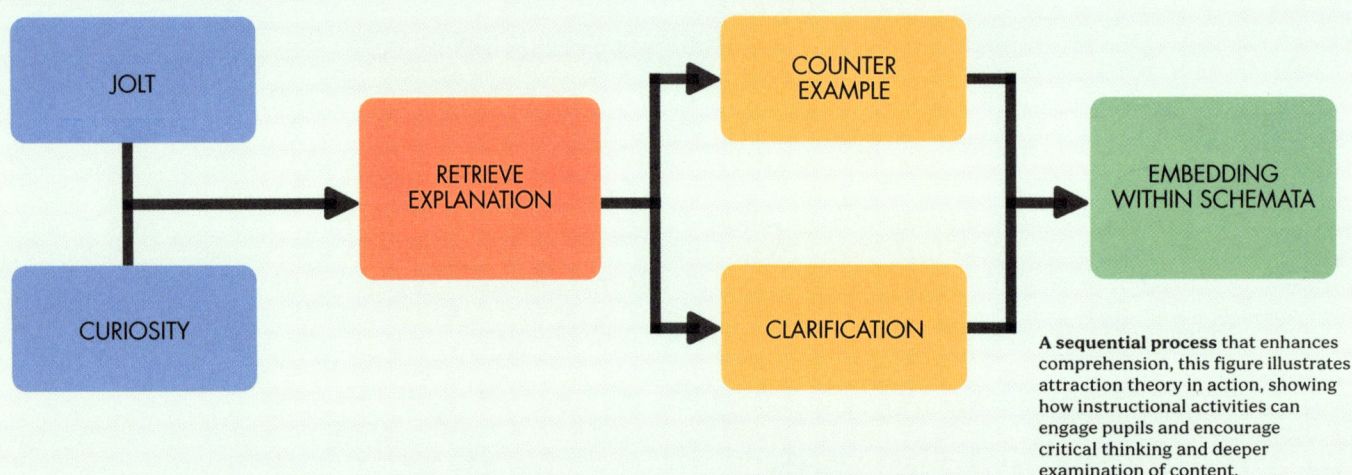

A sequential process that enhances comprehension, this figure illustrates attraction theory in action, showing how instructional activities can engage pupils and encourage critical thinking and deeper examination of content.

Graphic organisers, such as story maps and Venn diagrams, are powerful tools to boost reading engagement by helping readers visualise and organise information.

ensures a personal pursuit is achieved. Encouraging all readers to set reading goals and incorporating book talks and collaborative discussions allow pupils to learn from their peers and be positioned as knowledge leaders from their reading. Building communities of readers can revolutionise one's classroom, as pupils come together in shared discoveries of content and joint experiences shaped from their own input and feedback.

Daily reading habits become ritualistic; they are second nature in contexts that promote reading engagement. No matter a person's age, they can be established, maintained and enhanced over time. A minimum of 15 minutes is a strong start with ideal durations of 45 minutes or more (Duke & Carlisle, 2010).

Emotional factors

Curiosity is unfortunately often stymied beginning early on in formal schooling. We tell pupils to stop playing, talking, moving around and exploring; instead, we demand they silently read, do activity sheets and don't speak in class. We lead them to be uninterested in the concept of schooling, as it may feel contrived and contrary to their innate tendencies to examine the world around them.

Reading instruction has the potential to align with pupils' desire for choice and autonomy through the exploration of literary works and related investigations. Even the most resistant readers are curious about something. Therefore, there is a book or some type of reading material for everyone. Having access to diverse genres and various text types across multimodal formats is essential so that classrooms mimic the world outside those confines.

Teachers can also assess pupils' experiential base to learn what background information should be explicitly taught as part of the lesson. Leveraging what pupils have experienced and/or events of personal relevance keeps pupils engaged in classroom discussions and reading activities. Reading engagement is central to both the Science of Reading and best practices in reading instruction.

Reading Multisyllabic Words

by Jake Downs

Big words are everywhere in text. Effective strategies for teaching multisyllabic words are essential for reading success.

> BY THIRD GRADE, **65%** OF NEW WORDS PUPILS READ ARE MULTISYLLABIC, AND THIS DEMAND INCREASES THROUGH EARLY ADOLESCENCE

In first grade (Year 2) text in the US, one in every six words contains more than one syllable (Hiebert et al., 2020). By third grade (Year 4), 65% of new words pupils read are multisyllabic (Kearns & Hiebert, 2022), and this demand increases through early adolescence, where texts contain words with three or more syllables and multiple morphemes. These big words often carry key vocabulary and concepts essential for understanding. It's not surprising, then, that most pupils who struggle with comprehension on the National Assessment of Educational Progress (NAEP) also have difficulty reading multisyllabic words (Hiebert, 2022). Teaching

pupils to read complex, multisyllabic words is crucial for supporting comprehension (cf. Mesmer, 2024).

The challenge of reading multisyllabic words

Reading multisyllabic words can be challenging for readers of all grade levels. The most straightforward reason is that, by their nature, big words are longer and present a heavier decoding load for the reader (Heggie & Wade-Wooley, 2017). However, big words also add to this load in other ways. For instance, longer words often contain shifts in pronunciation between various forms of the word, such as in *nature* and *natural* or *sympathy* and *sympathetic* (Weber, 2018). These shifts typically involve the schwa sound ("ə", as in the last sound of *banana*) near the end of the word. Language challenges are also present in big words because pupils are more likely to encounter words for which they have varied or little understanding (Tortorelli et al., 2024).

Teaching pupils to read multisyllabic words

Evidence suggests that teaching pupils a flexible strategy to break words into smaller chunks can be productive for their word reading skills (Colenbrander et al., 2024; Kearns et al., 2022; Strong et al., 2024). One recent study (Downs, 2024; Downs et al., manuscript in preparation) included the following steps:

Identify known word parts
(i.e. circle known prefixes and suffixes).

Chunk the rest of the word
(i.e. underline the remaining vowels).

Blend the chunks of the word.

Check if the word is a real word and makes sense.

In this study, pupils practised this approach with three words per day. Each word was selected from daily reading based on its contribution to text meaning or if it contained a high-frequency syllable pattern.

The following routine was used to teach pupils how to read long words: Teachers modeled for pupils how to break apart each of the three words using the long word strategy. Pupils mimicked the strategy by breaking apart the words as a group and individually. The teacher and pupils would chorally read each phrase and sentence containing the target word from the text three times.

This routine occurred for five minutes per day. After, the group engaged in repeated reading of the text that contained the three target words. After 60 days, pupils demonstrated meaningful growth in their word reading accuracy.

What else helps?

Extensive, scaffolded practice in reading long words is essential for developing this skill. However, additional support can further help pupils read long words accurately and fluently. Common practices include teaching frequently occurring prefixes and suffixes, modelling and practising the spelling of multisyllabic words, spelling dictated sentences with these words, and introducing common syllable division patterns (Mesmer, 2024; Toste et al., 2017; Traga-Philipakkos et al., 2024).

Conclusion

Pupils must be able to read accurately to derive meaning from text. Even from the early primary school grades, big words comprise many of the words in texts. The demand of big words only increases as pupils advance through the reading levels. Accordingly, supporting pupil reading of multisyllabic words in strategic ways is an essential ingredient for promoting overall reading success.

Repeated Reading

by Jake Downs

Increasing the amount pupils read is a key part of developing proficient readers. Reading one text multiple times is one way to increase reading volume while improving fluency and comprehension.

Repeated reading has a long history in reading research. It has been shown to increase the fluency and comprehension of primary school pupils (Lee & Yoon, 2018).

Purposes for repeated reading

But although having pupils read a text or portion of a text multiple times seems simple, effective implementation may take creativity. To increase the relevance and impact of repeated reading, teachers should integrate instructional purposes with each read and add authenticity to repeated reading. Incorporating a comprehension goal with each read of a text is one way to integrate instructional purposes with repeated reading (Kunn, 2020).

Adding authenticity to repeated reading

One simple approach is to add a performance to the end of the repeated reading, as in reader's theatre. Reader's theatre provides pupils with multiple opportunities to read a text to the point of mastery and then perform that text to an audience (Young et al., 2019). Another recent approach to adding authenticity is called "Read Like Us" (Downs & Young, 2024). In this approach, pupils in small groups read a single short text five times in a single session and then "perform" the text to the paraprofessional instructor. Ultimately, teachers may find repeated reading to be more palatable for pupils when designed with authentic purposes in mind.

Reading texts repeatedly can help pupils target different skills and increase their reading volume, becoming stronger readers.

Text and Genre Study

Book Clubs and Literature Circles as Literacy Support	88
Reading Volume Strategies	90
Genre Study	92
Text Structure	94

Book Clubs and Literature Circles as Literacy Support

by L. Crosby-Guard

Literature circles and book clubs provide ways to support children's literacy along with other social and academic skills.

Book clubs and literature circles are choice-based discussion groups that support literacy and independent reading. Though they are similar, literature circles give pupils more structure. These groups' success depends on the educator setting the stage through preparation and planning.

Book clubs

Pupils participate in book clubs through discussion. The pupils are grouped based on which text they will read. Each group meets, discusses their assignments and disperses to read independently. The pupils read on their own, noting their connections to the text, developing discussion points and asking questions. Pupils then reconvene to talk about their ideas. This process occurs recursively until the pupils finish the text. Teachers will sometimes have the groups share reflections or create some product to express their experience of the text.

Anyone who works with children can see how this idealistic method can go awry. Book clubs require kids to work independently, prepare responsibly and collaborate effectively. In other words, book clubs require social and academic skills that may be underdeveloped

or non-existent in some pupils. Educators should then teach these skills with book clubs as an eventual goal. For example, educators can teach ways of annotating the text with questions and text connections before attempting a book club. Pupils can practise holding discussions through teacher-led small groups, whole-class discussions or think-pair-share activities. These smaller interactions, with teacher guidance and attention, can help pupils develop the skills needed to participate and learn in book clubs. Educators should plan by choosing the skills they would like pupils to show during book club and then teaching those skills over time before incorporating book clubs.

Educators can add more structure by providing pupils with a purpose for reading and discussion. For instance, one could instruct a book club to pick a character and track how the character changes throughout a chapter.

Literature circles

Some educators and pupils may need more structure than the general book club format would provide, and literature circles provide that structure. Literature circles are similar to book clubs in many ways. Pupil choice and participation propel the action, and pupils learn through discussion. The biggest difference between book clubs and literature circles is that in literature circles, pupils have defined jobs. Each pupil is responsible for a specific part of the discussion, and they complete their independent reading with their role in mind.

- **Discussion leader:** develops guiding questions and topics
- **Time keeper:** makes sure the group stays on task and that everyone speaks
- **Passage selector:** chooses a passage for the group to read closely and discuss
- **Vocabulary finder:** chooses unfamiliar or theme-related words for the group to analyse

When pupils are new to literature circles, the activity might not sound like much of a discussion at first. However, as they learn to prepare thoroughly and become more comfortable with the process, they will flow in and out of conversation more naturally.

Connections to the Science of Reading

Scarborough's Reading Rope (*see pages 14–17*) shows a visual metaphor for the multiple components of literacy, but the five major components – known as the five pillars of literacy – are phonics, fluency, vocabulary, reading comprehension and phonemic awareness. Literature circles and book clubs support many of these components. Through oral reading of select passages, pupils support each other's fluency, phonics and phonemic awareness. Vocabulary, phonemic awareness and phonics are enhanced as the pupils discuss the words they chose from the text. Discussing their various viewpoints and turning to each other for answers to their questions about a text improve pupils' reading comprehension.

> **"Each pupil is responsible for a specific part of the discussion."**

Reading Volume Strategies

by Jake Downs

Reading volume plays a pivotal role in developing proficient readers by fostering fluency, expanding vocabulary and building background knowledge. Teachers can implement effective strategies to increase pupils' reading volume.

Extended practice is essential for the development of expertise in any skill area, including reading. The extended reading required to become an expert reader is termed reading volume. Reading volume is important for two primary reasons. One is that reading volume facilitates becoming more efficient at reading text over time. As less cognition is required to process text, more cognitive bandwidth is available to make meaning in the text (LaBerge & Samuels, 1974) The other is that reading volume allows pupils to encounter sophisticated text with rare words (Hiebert, 2024). Given that even children's books contain more sophisticated language than conversations among adults (Hayes & Ahrens, 1988), reading volume is a viable approach to developing pupils' academic language.

Can reading volume replace reading instruction?

Although the concept of reading volume – the total amount of connected text one reads over a given period – is simple, its relationship to other important aspects of reading is complex. Volume is influenced by various factors, such as text complexity, instructional context and pupil engagement or interest in the text, which are, in turn, intricately linked to the reader's level of reading proficiency (Brenner & Hiebert, 2010). So, while sufficient reading volume provides pupils time to hone and refine their reading skills, the volume should complement high-quality reading instruction scaffolded by an expert teacher.

Increasing reading volume in the classroom

Fortunately, increasing reading volume is very doable for teachers. Two viable overarching principles exist for increasing reading volume in the classroom. Teachers must either structure opportunities to include more texts in the classroom or find reasons to read texts (or selections thereof) multiple times.

Including more texts

Studies indicate the amount of connected text reading included in popular core reading programmes is paltry (Brenner & Hiebert, 2010) and should be supplemented. Further, text reading is a critical component to building the background knowledge essential for success in the content areas.

Resources such as readworks.org or textproject.org have a range of texts of varying complexities that could readily supplement existing classroom texts. The large language models of modern AI can also create texts custom-tailored to the context and learning goals of classrooms (DeJulio et al., 2024).

Teachers may feel as though their instructional day is already jam-packed and may wonder where additional text can fit into a busy schedule. One recommendation is to find areas to "trim the fat" and replace low-leverage activities such as activity sheets or other decontextualised practices to make room for increasing reading volume.

Reading texts multiple times

Repeated reading has a long history in reading research and has been shown to increase the fluency and comprehension of elementary age pupils (Lee & Yoon, 2018). Incorporating a comprehension goal with each read of a text is one way to integrate instructional purposes with repeated reading (Kunn, 2020). For example, a short text on tectonic plates could be read once a day for four days. On the first day, pupils read the whole text but are expected to summarise the part of the text on divergent plates. Days two and three repeat this process, except pupils focus on convergent and transformative plates for each day. Finally, on day four, pupils compare and contrast the three plate types.

Repeated Reading

ALTHOUGH HAVING PUPILS READ A TEXT OR PORTION OF A TEXT MULTIPLE TIMES SEEMS SIMPLE, EFFECTIVE IMPLEMENTATION MAY TAKE CREATIVITY.

To increase the relevance and impact of repeated reading, teachers should integrate instructional purposes with each read and/ or add authenticity to repeated reading.

Adding authenticity is another way to structure pupil engagement during repeated reading (Young et al., 2022). One simple approach is to add a performance to the end of the repeated reading. Reader's theatre provides pupils with multiple opportunities to read a text to the point of mastery and then perform that text for an audience (Young et al., 2019). Another recent approach to adding authenticity is called "Read Like Us" (Downs & Young, 2024). In this approach, pupils in small groups read a single short text five times in a single session and then "perform" the text for the paraprofessional instructor.

Conclusion

While increasing the amount of reading is crucial, it must be a complement to high-quality reading instruction. Effective strategies for increasing reading volume in the classroom include strategically incorporating more texts into the curriculum and creatively finding reasons to read the same text more than once. By implementing these strategies, teachers can create a rich and engaging reading environment that fosters the development of lifelong readers.

Genre Study

by Bethanie Pletcher

Understanding genre facilitates reading comprehension. By knowing the conventions of their genres, pupils can better understand a variety of texts.

When we think of the word *genre*, we tend to equate it with learning about fiction, nonfiction, and poetry. Moreover, we tend to think of the texts we read in school and were then tested on. However, genre is so much more than this simple definition. It encompasses all the forms and functions of texts we encounter in a single day (and how we think about what is considered a "text"). *Genre* refers to any "kind of literary or artistic work or a class of artistic endeavor that has a characteristic form or technique" (Fountas & Pinnell, 2012, p. 2).

The importance of genre study

Think about a primary school child, for instance. They wake up in the morning and might watch a cartoon that contains a narrative story about two characters. At school, they encounter a morning message in the form of a letter that their teacher has written. They write a folktale with a peer during writing time. During the science lesson, they read an informational text about reptiles. When they get home, they are allowed some time to play a game on a tablet and notice the subtitles and instructions within

Genres that children might encounter range from a science book about lizards to a fairy tale to a recipe or cookbook.

the game. This is just a small sample of the genres a child might encounter. It is imperative that educators and caretakers expose children to as many genres as possible.

Defining genres

There is no formal list of genres, as they change over time as new genres (for example, GIFs and memes) appear and old ones (for example, westerns and epic poetry) decrease in quantity (Gamble & Yates, 2008). There are also some genres that are "privileged" in schools (Mo, 2014), such as folktales, realistic fiction, poetry and biography. These privileged genres are usually those that are included on standardised reading comprehension tests. But we shouldn't limit our thinking to these genres and ones that appear in books. While exposing children to all kinds of genres, it is important want to allow their interests to guide the process of selecting genres to explore (Gibney, 2012).

What children should know

Ideally, young children should be reading and writing a variety of texts. Additionally, children need to explain the differences between these genres and determine their central idea, and they need to do this while using relevant vocabulary that corresponds with the genre. For example, when working with poetry, they will use words and phrases such as *stanza*, *line*, *metre* and *rhythm*.

How to conduct genre study

A tried-and-true method of teaching genres is called genre study, which builds children's excitement for the genre under study while the teacher and pupils work together to define it (Concannon-Gibney, 2018). Educators should immerse pupils in the genre by providing frequent opportunities to read and write in the genre. Educators can allow pupils to explore the genre's characteristics and, at the same time, provide some explicit teaching to ensure that pupils' understandings are accurate.

Steps for implementing genre study

Select a few examples of the genre. Personal narrative is a great place to begin genre study because children enjoy hearing real-life stories of others and writing about their own experiences. Share several examples of personal narratives, such as *Peter's Chair* by Ezra Jack Keats and *Granny and Bean* by Karen Hesse.

Read and reread these texts across a few days. Discuss the texts and begin to identify common characteristics. Perhaps discuss how the common characteristic of the "stretching" of a story is presented in each book.

Use the listed characteristics and their descriptions to form a definition of the genre. Children might produce the following definition of a personal narrative: A genre in which the author, through a central character, describes, in detail, one small moment of their life.

Revisit the texts and explicitly teach the genre's characteristics. Select a mentor text and demonstrate how the author stretched a small moment in time. As you read other texts in this genre, apply the definition to other texts and revise the definition as needed. As you tackle new genres, allow children to discover connections among them.

> **Genre**
> Any type of text, from a grocery list to a poem, has a genre with a common form or style.

Text Structure

by Bethanie Pletcher

Texts differ widely in their format and structure, so it is crucial that children understand the variety of text types. How they read the structure of each text will require different sets of skills.

On any given day, you may read an email, a recipe and a chapter of a fiction book. However, you will not read these texts in the same way — you will approach each one differently based on the text's structure. *Text structure* refers to the way an author organises and formats a piece of literature, whether narrative or non-narrative (Fountas & Pinnell, 2017). A narrative text typically follows a chronological storyline and includes a beginning, middle and end and can be fictional or biographical. A nonnarrative structure is typically used in informational texts. Children should have access to high-interest texts in many formats, including narrative texts with one storyline or multiple storylines, texts that change perspective within the narrative, and nonfiction texts with cause-and-effect, chronological and compare/contrast structures. What follows are descriptions of two text structures and an example of how to teach children to approach each to enhance their reading comprehension.

Sample graphic organiser: Fiction

Sample text: *Amazing Grace* by Mary Hoffman

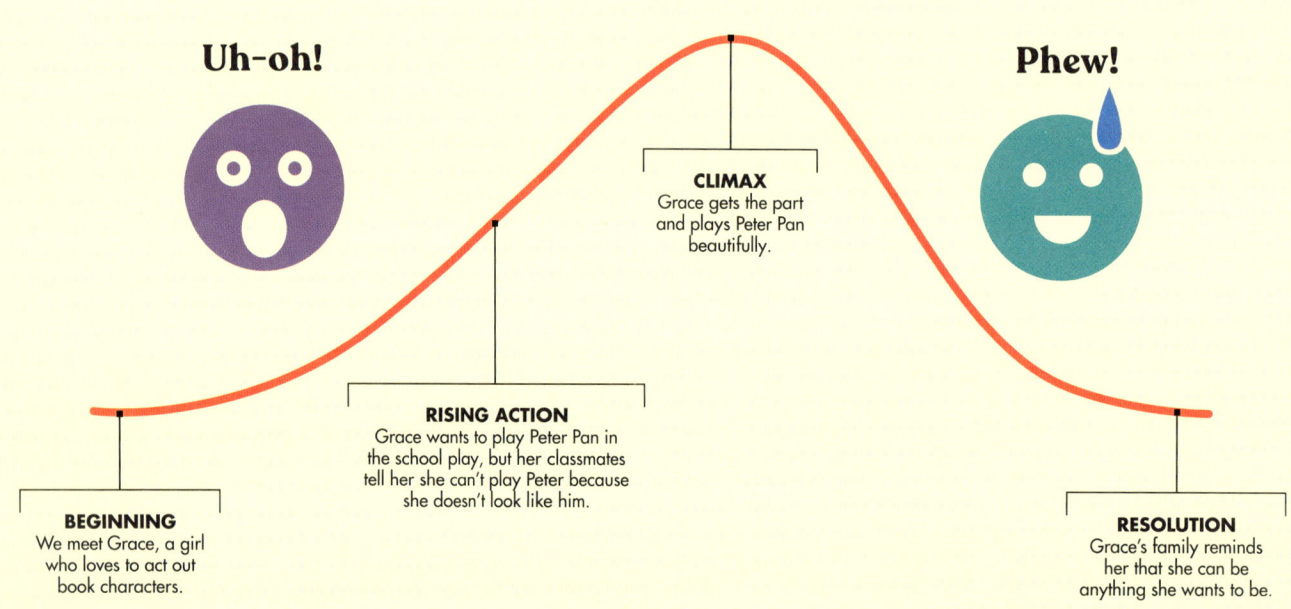

Uh-oh!

CLIMAX
Grace gets the part and plays Peter Pan beautifully.

Phew!

RISING ACTION
Grace wants to play Peter Pan in the school play, but her classmates tell her she can't play Peter because she doesn't look like him.

BEGINNING
We meet Grace, a girl who loves to act out book characters.

RESOLUTION
Grace's family reminds her that she can be anything she wants to be.

Sample graphic organiser: Nonfiction

Sample text: *What If You Had Animal Eyes!?* by Sandra Markle

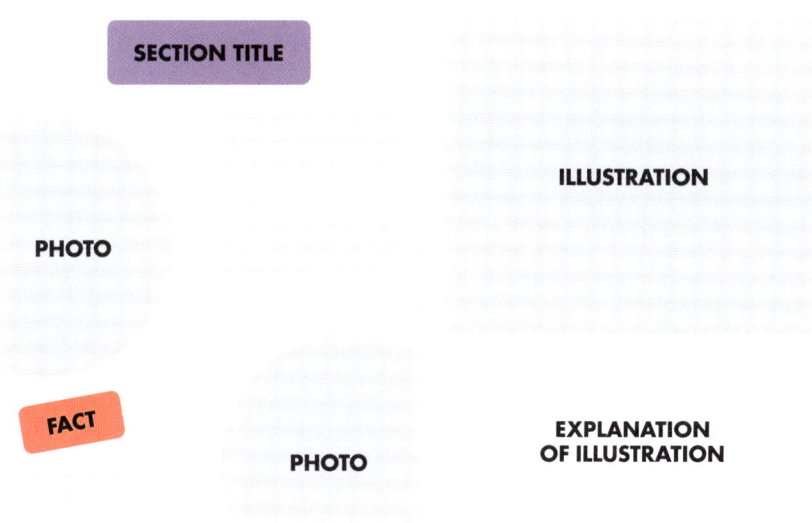

Fiction narrative texts with one storyline

The sequential narrative text structure is perhaps the most common type that is used in primary school classrooms, mainly due to its facilitation of story structure – a beginning that presents the setting and characters, a middle that presents a problem for the main character(s), and an ending where the problem is solved. Due to this structure, the reader begins at the front of the book and reads through to the end. One way to teach this text structure is by using a visual aid, such as the Uh-oh...Phew! graphic organiser at left (Seravallo, 2015). For example, after reading the book *Amazing Grace* (Hoffman, 1991), children can discuss and/or write about the beginning of the book while referring to the graphic organiser. Here, they will notice the rising action, the climax (the "uh-oh") and the resolution (the "phew").

Nonfiction informational texts divided into sections

Informational texts are varied in their format. An author may present information about a single topic and divide the book into sections to organise the contents. The reader does not necessarily have to read the book from front cover to back cover, since the information is usually not presented in sequential order. One technique for teaching this text type is the "Don't Skip It!" strategy (Duke, 2014). For example, *What If You Had Animal Eyes!?* (Markle, 2017) presents several challenges to the reader. Each two-page spread includes photographs, illustrations, a main text section and extra information at the bottom of each page in a "Facts" box. With a text such as this, it is imperative to pay attention to the text features on each page and not solely the main text.

Oral Language Development

The Science of Speaking in the Reading Brain	98
Pragmatics and Reading	100
The Science of Biliteracy Development	102
The Importance of Oral Language Development in Literacy	106
The Power of Language Play in Literacy Development	112
Semantics and Reading	115

The Science of Speaking in the Reading Brain

by L. Crosby-Guard

Despite the assumption that speaking and reading are separate skills, the Science of Reading proves that we use speaking skills as we read. The parts of our brains that we use to speak help us to pronounce and sound out words.

What role does speaking play in reading? To understand the link between reading and speaking, remember that reading is not an innate or natural skill. There is no "reading centre" in the brain as there is for sight, for instance. Humans have learned to engage various parts of the brain simultaneously to gain the ability to read. In this way, the brain uses speech and language processes to enable reading.

How speaking becomes reading in the brain

The process of learning to read starts with learning to speak, strengthening the parts of our brains used for oral language. The parts of the brain needed to learn to speak are ready for use at birth and learning how to speak makes them stronger. These parts of the brain grow, and pupils start to gain the ability to associate letters with letter sounds. Typically, children are in preschool as this takes place. Educators and parents help this process along by offering explicit phonics instruction and practice. Yes, teaching children to read helps to change and grow their young brains! As pupils grow older and get further phonics and phonemic instruction, they learn more ways to use letters to make words. No matter how automatically a pupil can recognise a word, their brain is still actively processing connections between sounds and letters.

Speaking also helps with comprehension and vocabulary acquisition. Many people hear new words before they read them for the first time. The speaking parts of the brain help them understand oral language and ascertain the gist of what is said. These same parts of the brain help to understand how words work together in sentences to make meaning. As pupils strengthen their reading, they can more quickly recognise letters, associate the letters with sounds, combine them to make words and understand what words mean in context of a sentence. When a pupil pronounces each phoneme in a CVC (consonant-vowel-consonant) word or uses context clues to understand *minute* (very small) versus *minute* (60 seconds), they are using some of the same parts of the brain that they use for speaking.

How to use speech to aid reading

One of the easiest and most accessible ways to help a child read is to read to them. This is common advice because children benefit in multiple ways from being read to aloud. Reading aloud helps children link sounds to letters in their brains. Unfortunately, many adults stop reading to children as they get older, but the benefits of being read to aloud do not cease with age. Older children benefit from hearing fluent reading and from watching adults make and correct reading errors.

Schools can help children link reading and speech by providing consistent and ongoing phonics instruction, especially in early childhood classrooms. For a time, popular reading instruction taught pupils to read by recognising whole words at once. However, research has shown that this is not the way that reading occurs in the brain. The brain needs to connect letters with sounds and needs to do so quickly. Phonics instruction helps children learn to quickly make words with the letters they see. That way, they can focus more on meaning and comprehension, as higher grades will require them to do. Thus, schools must provide pupils with the opportunity to master phonics and must employ interventions to strengthen these skills while pupils are young.

Reading and the brain

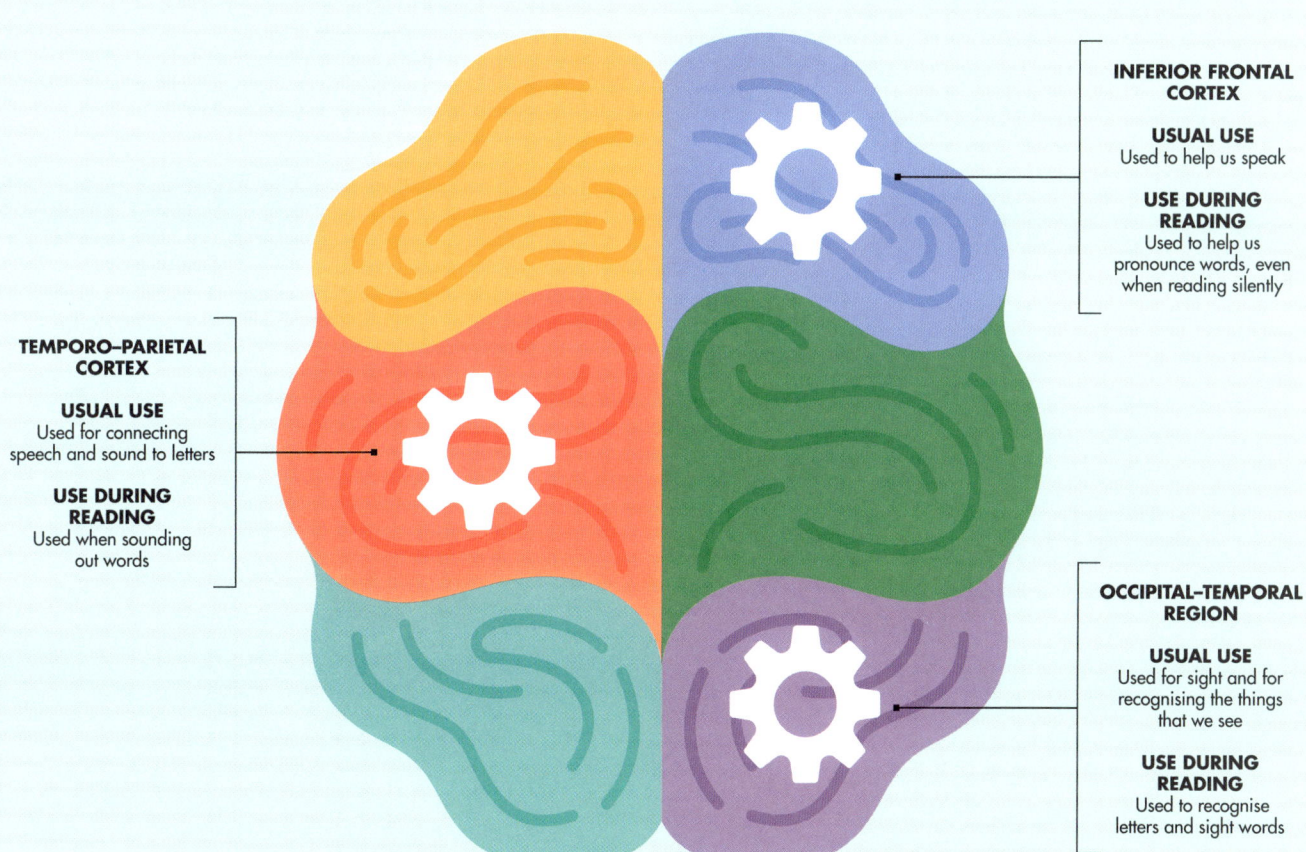

TEMPORO–PARIETAL CORTEX

USUAL USE
Used for connecting speech and sound to letters

USE DURING READING
Used when sounding out words

INFERIOR FRONTAL CORTEX

USUAL USE
Used to help us speak

USE DURING READING
Used to help us pronounce words, even when reading silently

OCCIPITAL–TEMPORAL REGION

USUAL USE
Used for sight and for recognising the things that we see

USE DURING READING
Used to recognise letters and sight words

Pragmatics and Reading

by Lori Fromowitz

Pragmatics is the use of language across contexts, which can impact a learner's ability to master basic reading concepts and comprehend written text.

Language has several components, including phonemics (the sounds of speech), semantics (word meaning), morphology (the forms of words) and syntax (sentence structure). Pragmatics is the application of all of these components as well as the unstated aspects of language (nonliteral language, tone of voice, facial expressions and body language, interpretation of emotion, perspective and problem-solving). Pragmatics may be defined as the ability to share and understand the message across contexts. Social language, one piece of pragmatics, is impacted by a person's communication partner and other factors, such as time and movement through space.

Pragmatics and reading comprehension

Reading mastery is a result of the ability to decode text into words and comprehend the words' meaning. Pragmatics plays a part both in learning to decode and in reading comprehension. Pragmatic skills can also impact writing, particularly as the skills relate to writers' ability to understand a reader's perspective.

Reading comprehension is dependent on pupils applying context, including interpreting multiple-meaning words and nonliteral language, such as metaphors. Reading comprehension may prove to be more difficult for pupils who are autistic or have pragmatic language disorders (Freed et al., 2011). Pupils who have pragmatic language disorders may have difficulty in social situations and may benefit from intervention that also supports their communication preferences (Burch, 2023).

Fluency, which is a predictor of reading comprehension, has three components: accuracy, rate and expression. Therefore, reading comprehension is in part dependent on prosody (intonation), which is one facet of pragmatic language (Puranik et al., 2008).

Difficulties with underlying forms and meaning of language can also impact pragmatic language skills. But individuals with average or above average underlying language ability may still present with difficulties or differences with pragmatics. Though pragmatics limitations or

---

Pragmatics and Culture

PRAGMATICS VARIES WIDELY ACROSS LANGUAGE AND CULTURE.

It may extend to how you speak to different people, what volume you use or whether you make eye contact when talking. Such variation should not be interpreted as a disability but should be taken into account when teaching reading to English language learners and readers across cultures.

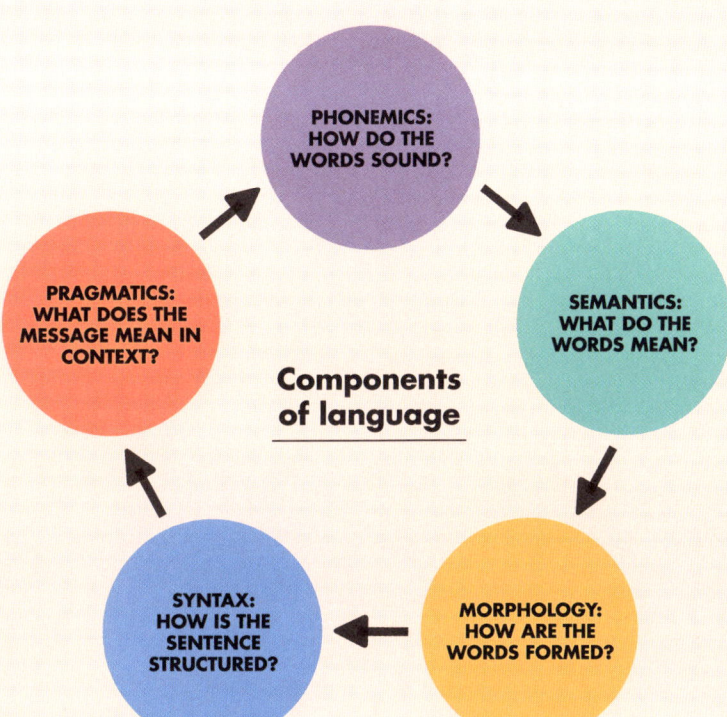

Components of language

differences are often part of an autism profile, many pupils will demonstrate pragmatics variations in the absence of autism.

Executive function, pragmatics and the written expression link

Executive function is the planner in your brain that helps you organise. Executive functions include the ability to self-monitor, inhibit, self-regulate, plan, organise and be mentally flexible. Pragmatic language and executive function are interdependent (Blain-Brière et al., 2014). Individuals with executive function challenges may have difficulty attending to and processing speech sounds (Puranik et al., 2008) and attending to shared messages. This can translate into difficulty interpreting written text (Puranik et al., 2008). Individuals who have poor executive function may also have difficulty planning and organising their writing effectively (Soto et al., 2021).

Intervention

When working with pupils who have pragmatic language disabilities, consider the following strategies:

- explicitly teach nonliteral language
- diagram cause and effect in texts
- identify times when prosody may change
- discuss author's purpose and perspective
- make inferences and predictions

If a pupil demonstrates difficulty with pragmatics in spoken and written language, consider working with a speech language pathologist.

The Science of Biliteracy Development

by Alta Joy Broughton, PhD

The science of biliteracy development examines the complementary features of the Science of Reading with research on the cognitive processes and linguistic features of becoming bilingual.

As school communities around the world diversify, bilingual education has increased in popularity. Designing effective biliteracy instruction requires the interplay of what we know about how the brain learns language and linguistic features of the additional language. New research about developing biliteracy helps show how it connects to the principles of the Science of Reading.

Biliteracy development is the acquisition of oral language in concert with the phonological and written system of two or more languages (Grosjean, 2013). Some people might presume that biliteracy requires double the effort to learn two of everything, but the principles of bilingualism actually demonstrate how literacy in one language can complement and support literacy in another language.

There are four foundational concepts to biliteracy:

All languages are equally complex and include similar components. No single language is more "difficult" to learn than another (Joseph & Newmeyer, 2012).

Bilingual speakers are not simply two monolingual speakers in one. Bilinguals draw from an integrated complex adaptive system (Filipović et al. 2019; García & Kleifgen, 2018; Kroll & Bialyst, 2013).

Developing fluency in one language strengthens fluency in the other, in a principle known as linguistic interdependence (Cummins, 1981).

Skills in different languages are connected to a Common Underlying Proficiency. This means that knowledge and abilities acquired in one language are applicable to the additional language (Cummins, 1991).

The first concept supports the view that all learners can become bilingual with the appropriate instruction. Understanding the linguistic similarities and differences of languages has important implications for teaching phonological awareness. All spoken languages use a system of sounds to construct words. Some languages construct word meanings only with syllables and phonemes, while other languages also use a tonal system. English, Korean, Japanese, Germanic, Greek and Latin-based languages are examples of phonetic languages. In these languages, words are constructed from a system of syllables and phonemes, and the written spelling closely aligns with spoken pronunciation. When teaching phonemic awareness, phonics and decoding, educators can make acquiring the additional language seem "easier" by drawing connections between the similarities of English and another phonetic language.

The second concept asserts that bilinguals acquire additional languages by integrating the new language into one system. As a result, biliteracy instruction should support pupils

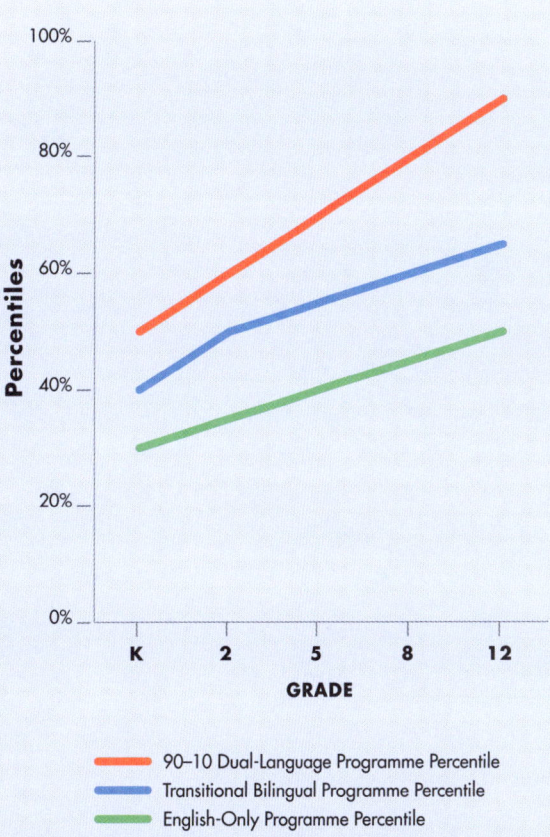

This graph compares the percentile ranks of pupil performance in reading across three types of educational programmes: 90–10 Dual–Language Programmes, Transitional Bilingual Programmes and English-Only Programmes. Percentile ranks were collected at key grade levels (K, 2, 5, 8 and 12) in the US. The data highlights the superior performance of pupils in dual-language programmes, demonstrating a consistent upward trend compared to their peers in transitional and English-only programmes.

> **"Bilingual speakers are not two monolingual speakers in one. They use an integrated, adaptive system."**

to use all their linguistic resources to learn new content (Broughton et al., 2023). This concept has important conclusions for teaching vocabulary and comprehension when reading aloud to children as well as reading connected text. Teachers can support the development of this integrated system through explicit instruction. Vocabulary acquisition is supported through drawing associations between true cognates (e.g., *bicycle/bicicleta* or *confusión/confusion*) and distinguishing false cognates (e.g., *librería* in Spanish: bookshop vs. *library* in English: library) (Calderón et al., 2003). Teachers can also support comprehension by encouraging pupils to recall information in both languages to build comprehension of new content, known as "translanguaging" (García & Kleifgen, 2018).

Mutual benefits of languages

The third concept explains how the learning of a home language (L1) and an additional language (L2) is mutually beneficial (Cummins, 1981). By increasing their cognitive and linguistic capacity in their home language, children have the foundation to acquire similar capacities in the additional language. This hypothesis is supported by the strong, long-term academic achievement of English learners who received biliteracy instruction versus those who received English-only literacy instruction. Therefore, coordinated, simultaneous reading instruction in both languages will yield the best outcomes for all pupils.

The fourth concept, Common Underlying Proficiency, explains that when languages share similar features, children transfer skills across languages. Studies of preschoolers' phonological awareness in English and Spanish demonstrate that children have similar skills in both languages. Therefore, researchers believe that when there is substantial overlap in code-related skills, such as letter names and letter-sound correspondence, across languages (as is the case for English and Spanish), children will apply knowledge gained from the language of instruction to their other language (Goodrich & Lonigan, 2017). This is true even when letter names and letter-sound correspondence may not have been explicitly taught. This supports the principle of explicit instruction to teach content that occurs more frequently first. Biliteracy instruction must look across both languages to determine high-frequency letter-sounds and words.

In conclusion, though many questions remain about how the brain learns to read in an additional language, applying an asset-based perspective will ensure all pupils can reap the benefits of bilingualism.

Underlying proficiency
Shared features help children apply skills across multiple languages.

Cummins' language interdependence model for biliteracy

Visible Literacy Skills

LETTER KNOWLEDGE
PHONOLOGICAL AWARENESS
READING FLUENCY
LANGUAGE USE

Common Underlying Proficiency

Literacy Skills and Strategies

LISTENING SKILLS
VOCABULARY STRATEGIES
READING COMPREHENSION
ABILITY TO MAKE INFERENCES

Both a pupil's home language (L1) and an additional language (L2) are united by a Common Underlying Proficiency. These aspects under the "surface" may be learned in one language, but strengthen fluency in both languages.

The Importance of Oral Language Development in Literacy

by Alexis Quinn Robinson

Oral language skills provide a foundation for reading and writing. Caregivers and educators can use strategies to support oral language development and foster early literacy.

Oral language development is a critical component of early literacy and overall academic success. It encompasses the skills and knowledge that children need to understand and use spoken language effectively. These skills form the foundation for reading and writing, making oral language development a key focus in early childhood education.

Understanding oral language development

Oral language development involves several interconnected skills, including listening, speaking, vocabulary, grammar and comprehension. These skills develop through interactions with caregivers, teachers and peers, as well as through exposure to rich language environments.

Listening and speaking: These are the primary modes of communication for young children. Listening skills involve the ability to understand and process spoken language, while speaking skills involve the ability to express thoughts and ideas clearly. Both are essential for effective communication and are developed through everyday conversations and interactions.

Vocabulary: A robust vocabulary is crucial for both oral and written language. Children learn new words through direct instruction and incidental learning during conversations and reading. A strong vocabulary helps children understand what they hear and read, and it enables them to express themselves more precisely.

Grammar: Understanding the rules of language, such as syntax and morphology, is essential for constructing meaningful sentences. Children learn grammar through exposure to correct language models and through practice in speaking and writing.

Comprehension: This involves the ability to understand and interpret spoken language. Comprehension skills are developed through listening to stories, engaging in discussions, and asking and answering questions.

Rich language environment
Surround pupils with language and give them opportunities to use it.

ORAL LANGUAGE DEVELOPMENT 107

The role of oral language in literacy

Oral language skills are the foundation upon which reading and writing are built. Here's how these skills impact literacy development:

Phonological awareness: This is the ability to recognise and manipulate the sounds of spoken language. It is a critical precursor to reading, as it helps children understand that words are made up of individual sounds (phonemes). Activities like rhyming, clapping out syllables and playing with sounds can enhance phonological awareness.

Reading comprehension: Strong oral language skills support reading comprehension. Children who have a rich vocabulary and good listening comprehension are better able to understand and make meaning from the texts they read. They can draw on their oral language knowledge to infer, predict and summarise information.

Writing skills: Oral language development also influences writing. Children who can express their thoughts clearly in spoken language are better equipped to do so in writing. They can use their vocabulary and understanding of grammar to construct coherent and detailed written texts.

Phoneme manipulation
Help pupils recognise sounds by adding, deleting or replacing phonemes in words.

Strategies for promoting oral language development

Educators and caregivers can use various strategies to support and enhance oral language development in children:

Interactive read-alouds: Reading books aloud to children and engaging them in discussions about the story can significantly boost their oral language skills. Ask open-ended questions, encourage predictions and discuss new vocabulary words.

Rich language environment: Create an environment where children are exposed to a wide range of vocabulary and language structures. Use descriptive language, model correct grammar, and introduce new words in context.

Conversations and discussions: Engage children in meaningful conversations throughout the day. Encourage them to share their thoughts, ask questions and express their ideas. Listen actively and respond thoughtfully to their contributions.

Storytelling and narratives: Encourage children to tell their own stories and share personal experiences. This helps them practise organising their thoughts, using descriptive language and understanding narrative structure.

Play-based learning: Incorporate language-rich activities into play. Role-playing, puppet shows and pretend play provide opportunities for children to use and expand their oral language skills in a fun and engaging way.

Songs and rhymes: Enhance phonological awareness and vocabulary through the repetitive and rhythmic nature of songs and rhymes.

Conclusion

Oral language development is a vital aspect of early literacy and overall academic success. Through intentional and engaging strategies, we can support children in becoming confident and effective communicators, setting them on a path to lifelong learning and achievement.

"**Oral language development is a vital aspect of early literacy and overall academic success**".

> "Assessments should be accessible and equitable, helping all pupils access, comprehend and demonstrate their knowledge."

Alison Divino Driscoll

The Power of Language Play in Literacy Development

by Alexis Quinn Robinson

Research shows that language play provides a powerful way to support literacy. Puns, word games and rhymes can help educators incorporate language play into everyday activities.

Language play, the creative and playful use of language, is a powerful tool in literacy development. It involves manipulating sounds, words and sentences in fun and imaginative ways, helping children develop essential language and literacy skills. From rhymes and riddles to puns and word games, language play engages children in a joyful exploration of language, fostering a love for words and reading.

Understanding language play

Language play can take many forms, including these:

Phonological play involves playing with the sounds of language. Activities like rhyming, alliteration and tongue twisters help children become aware of the sounds within words, an essential skill for reading and spelling. For example, saying "Sally sells seashells by the seashore" helps children focus on the /s/ sound.

Morphological play involves manipulating the structure of words. Children might create new words by adding prefixes or suffixes, or by blending two words together (e.g., "brunch" from "breakfast" and "lunch"). This type of play helps children understand how words are formed and how they can be modified to change meaning.

Syntactic play involves experimenting with sentence structure. Children might create silly sentences by rearranging words or by using unconventional grammar. For example, "The cat danced on the moon" is a playful way to explore sentence construction and meaning.

Semantic play involves playing with the meanings of words. Puns, jokes and riddles are common forms of semantic play. For instance, the joke "Why did the scarecrow win an award? Because he was outstanding in his field!" plays with the multiple meanings of "outstanding".

The benefits of language play

Engaging in language play offers numerous benefits for literacy development:

Phonological awareness: Language play enhances phonological awareness, the ability to recognise and manipulate the sounds of language. This skill is crucial for learning to read and spell. Rhyming games, for example, help children notice sound patterns and develop an ear for phonemes.

Vocabulary development: Through language play, children are exposed to new words and their meanings. Playing with words in different

Word games and puzzles help children think about words and their structures.

contexts helps children understand and remember them better. For example, creating silly sentences with new vocabulary words makes learning them more enjoyable and memorable.

Creativity and imagination: Language play encourages creativity and imagination. Children learn to think outside the box and experiment with language in novel ways. This creative exploration fosters a love for language and reading, making literacy activities more engaging and enjoyable.

Critical thinking: Solving riddles and understanding puns requires critical thinking and problem-solving skills. Children learn to think about language in different ways, considering multiple meanings and interpretations. This analytical thinking is beneficial for reading comprehension and overall cognitive development.

Social interaction: Language play often involves social interaction, whether it's telling jokes, playing word games or creating stories together. These interactions help children develop communication skills, learn to take turns and understand different perspectives.

Strategies for incorporating language play

Educators and caregivers can incorporate language play into daily activities to support literacy development:

Read aloud with expression: Reading books with expressive voices and playful language can captivate children's attention and make reading fun. Choose books with rhymes, alliteration and wordplay to highlight the playful aspects of language.

Play word games: Engage children in word games like Scrabble®, Boggle® or word searches. These games encourage children to think about words and their structures, enhancing vocabulary and spelling skills.

Create rhymes and songs: Encourage children to create their own rhymes and songs. This activity helps them play with sounds and rhythms, developing phonological awareness and a love for language.

Tell jokes and riddles: Share jokes and riddles with children to stimulate their thinking and understanding of word meanings. Encourage them to come up with their own jokes and riddles to practise semantic play.

Encourage storytelling: Provide opportunities for children to tell their own stories. Use prompts or picture cards to inspire creativity. Storytelling helps children practise syntactic play and develop narrative skills.

Use tongue twisters: Challenge children with tongue twisters to practise phonological play. This fun activity helps them focus on articulation and sound patterns.

Conclusion

Language play is a powerful and enjoyable way to support literacy development. By engaging in the playful and creative use of language, children develop essential skills, such as phonological awareness, vocabulary, creativity, critical thinking and social interaction. Incorporating language play into daily activities can make learning to read and write a joyful and enriching experience, laying a strong foundation for lifelong literacy and a love for language.

Semantics and Reading

by Trina Gould Williams

Semantics, or understanding word meanings, is essential for proficient reading. It helps us recognise words, understand context and connect language skills in the brain. Knowing about semantics can help teachers improve reading instruction.

Semantics is a key aspect of the study of linguistics. Every day we use semantics when we talk to others or consider what they say to us. But how can we help pupils use semantics to boost their reading comprehension?

To understand why semantics is so important for reading, it helps to look at some big ideas about how we learn to read. Two helpful models are Scarborough's Reading Rope (*see pages 14–17*) and the Simple View of Reading (*see pages 12–13*). Both show that good readers need two main abilities: the ability to recognise words easily and to understand what those words mean. Semantics, along with grammar (syntax), how we use language in different situations (pragmatics) and understanding longer stretches of text (discourse), falls under the "understanding language" part of reading. So, while these models might organise the parts of reading a little differently, they agree that semantics is a key ingredient for becoming a skilled reader.

More than just dictionary meanings: It's about nuance

Semantics isn't just about knowing dictionary definitions. It's about understanding how words work in real life. It's about the subtle differences between words. *Frugal* and *stingy*, for example, both might be used to describe a person who is reluctant to spend money. But one word has a much more positive connotation than the other. Understanding these "degrees" of meaning helps us not only understand what we read but also write more effectively. It helps us grasp the full richness of language.

Semantics and reading development: From sounds to meaning

Kids start learning about words by hearing them spoken. As they learn to read, they begin to connect those spoken words to written letters. There is a natural progression from linking sounds to letters to linking those letters to meanings. When teachers directly teach about word meanings (explicit instruction), it helps kids understand how the context of a sentence or even a whole paragraph can change the meaning of a word. For example, the word *bank* can be used as a noun for the side of a river (*We waited on the bank to board the canoe*) or verb meaning to keep or store (*I banked all my hopes on the effort*), among other meanings. The surrounding words help us understand which meaning is intended.

The Science of Reading and semantics: Putting it all together

Understanding word meanings is essential for getting information from what we read. Instructional practices associated with the Science of Reading support this idea in several ways:

Explicit vocabulary instruction: Teachers directly teach new words, including their definitions and how to use them in different situations. This isn't just about memorising definitions; it's about understanding how words function in context. Reading comprehension requires the reader to recognise an author's perspective and purpose as well as identify the motivations and perspectives of characters. By understanding the nuance of how authors and characters use words, readers can better understand and respond to texts.

Semantic mapping: This is a visual way to explore the relationships between words. It involves creating diagrams or webs that show how different words are connected by meaning. This helps kids build a deeper understanding of vocabulary and how words relate to each other. One example of a semantic map is a semantic gradient or continuum, which can show subtle differences between words – from weaker to stronger meanings. See the graphic to the right for an example. Words such as *hot, humid, arid,*

"Semantics isn't just about knowing dictionary definitions. It's about understanding how words work in real life".

sweltering and *boiling* all have similar meanings, but with important distinctions. Skilled readers grasp the distinctions between these terms and their effects on the meaning of a text.

Semantics and reading growth

In short, semantics is about the meanings of words and phrases as well as how words relate to each other within a sentence and how context influences the interpretation. Understanding word meanings is crucial for reading comprehension and is a key focus of effective reading instruction based on scientific research.

Semantics is essential to a developing and even proficient reader's ability to comprehend, express themselves effectively and think critically. Providing explicit instruction on semantics and daily opportunities to explore language will contribute greatly to a reader's growth and proficiency.

Semantics and Pragmatics

BOTH SEMANTICS AND PRAGMATICS ARE KEY ELEMENTS OF LANGUAGE AND COMMUNICATION.
Semantics mainly involves what words, phrases and sentences mean. Pragmatics focuses more on the social context that affects the meaning of the words, phrases and sentences.

Semantics can involve understanding subtle differences between words. For example, **hot** and **sweltering** both describe high temperatures, but *sweltering* suggests a much more intense heat.

Assessment and Intervention

Progress Monitoring with Reading Fluency Measures   120

Response to Intervention   122

Empowering Learning Through Formative Assessments   126

Three Tiers of Support for Pupils   129

Using DIBELS for Diagnostic Assessment   130

Evaluating Reading Through Summative Assessment   132

Progress Monitoring with Reading Fluency Measures

by Vidya Munandar, Zachary Johnson and Denise Ross

Progress monitoring is an assessment approach that provides teachers with valuable data on the effectiveness of their instruction and signals when to maintain or adjust instructional strategies.

Progress monitoring often centres on reading fluency, a critical component of skilled reading. Fluency measures both accuracy and speed to determine a pupil's reading rate. This practice is rooted in Ogden Lindsley's development of Precision Teaching, or PT (Lindsley, 1992), which emphasised the importance of response rate in learning. Contemporary reading research highlights the importance of fluency in mastering foundational skills, such as word-level reading and acquiring more advanced skills, like reading comprehension. Instructional strategies, such as repeated reading and passage previewing, can enhance both speed and accuracy for pupils needing support. Additionally, curriculum-based measures (CBMs) like the Dynamic Indicators of Basic Early Literacy Skills (DIBELS; Good et al., 2019) and AIMSweb (Pearson, 2012) have become essential tools for assessing and monitoring reading fluency. These tools provide reliable data that educators can use to tailor instruction. Progress monitoring can also encompass a variety of reading skills, including comprehension, writing, phonics, oral passage reading and word-reading fluency.

Key concepts in progress monitoring

Three foundational concepts in progress monitoring are baseline data, goal-setting and trends. Baseline data provide a clear starting point by assessing a pupil's performance before instruction begins. These data are collected through repeated measures and serve as a foundation for understanding a pupil's current performance before instruction.

For fluency instruction, teachers often use the median score from multiple assessments or analyse a trend from three or more data points to establish an accurate baseline.

Using baseline data, teachers then set measurable and attainable goals for the pupil. For example, a fourth-grade (Year 5) pupil in the US reading 75 correct words per minute (CWPM) is at the 25th percentile for their grade level in the fall, according to fluency norms (Hasbrouck & Tindal, 2017) and might be given an end-of-year goal of 94 CWPM to read at the 50th percentile. These goals ensure that progress is both realistic and challenging, helping pupils improve while giving teachers a clear target for instructional planning.

Baseline data
Information about each pupil's current reading level helps teachers set goals.

To monitor progress, teachers analyse trends by graphing pupil performance over time. An ascending or upward trend signifies improvement and validates the current instructional approach. Conversely, a flat or descending trend indicates a lack of progress, prompting the teacher to adjust their methods or introduce additional interventions.

Implementation of progress monitoring

Before instruction begins, teachers decide how frequently to measure progress. This can range from daily assessments integrated into lessons to weekly evaluations. Materials for progress monitoring can be created by converting reading level texts into fluency exercises or using pre-developed resources, such as DIBELS (*see pages 130–131*).

For fluency monitoring, progress is measured by calculating correct responses per minute, which involves subtracting the number of errors from the total responses. These data points are then plotted on a graph, allowing teachers to visualise the pupil's growth and make informed decisions about their instructional strategies.

Common interventions

Repeated reading where pupils practise the same passage more than once, and listening passage preview where pupils listen to the passage before reading it, are highly effective strategies that help pupils improve both speed and accuracy. Diagnosing specific errors during progress monitoring also allows teachers to provide targeted instruction for areas of difficulty. Additionally, teachers can involve pupils in the process through graphing their own data or reading aloud with a peer monitoring.

Benefits of progress monitoring

One of the most significant advantages of progress monitoring is the early identification of reading difficulties, which enables timely intervention and prevents small challenges from escalating into larger issues. Fluency measurement is another critical aspect, as it serves as a strong predictor of more complex reading skills, such as comprehension and automaticity in word recognition.

The visual analysis provided by graphing pupil data makes it simple for educators to identify trends and communicate progress to pupils, parents and other stakeholders. Finally, progress monitoring leads to improved reading outcomes when pupils receive the targeted support they need.

Educators can measure fluency by calculating the words per minute a pupil reads correctly.

Response to Intervention

by Morgan Sott

Response to Intervention is a process within the Multi-Tiered Systems of Support framework that uses data to pinpoint specific challenges for pupils.

Response to Intervention, or RTI, became federal law in the United States when the US Department of Education reauthorised the Individuals with Disabilities Education Act in 2004 (Allen-Manning, 2024). The primary purpose of RTI is to support all pupils through early identification and a tiered instruction approach.

RTI in reading has a major focus on foundational skills outlined in the body of research known as the Science of Reading. The RTI process focuses on delivering systematic, explicit instruction through layers of ongoing support.

Tiers of support

There are three tiers of support within the RTI process. All RTI pupils should move fluidly throughout the tiers when deemed appropriate. Note that the tiers build upon one another. By the time pupils reach tier 3, they would be receiving three layers of instructional support.

Tier 1: Core instruction: All pupils receive explicit reading instruction based on evidence-based practices. About 80% of pupils should respond proficiently to the core instruction.

Tier 2: Targeted intervention: Some pupils will not master the content through the core instruction. It is estimated that 10–15% of pupils will need additional targeted interventions to support their learning. Targeted interventions can occur a few times a week and usually take place in a small group setting. In order to identify which evidence-based intervention will be needed, the teacher or reading specialist must give a diagnostic assessment. Targeted interventions should be used for 4–6 weeks before reevaluating their effectiveness.

Tier 3: Intensive intervention: Very few pupils, around 5% or less, may need additional intensive intervention. This type of intervention is usually done in a one-on-one setting for a longer period of time.

"The RTI model, when aligned with the Science of Reading, offers a powerful process for addressing the diverse needs of learners."

Key principles for effective RTI implementation

Early identification: Universal screeners given at the beginning of the school year help identify pupils who may already struggle to read. Schools should screen pupils beginning as early as Reception. Research has shown that pupils who have difficulty learning to read are unlikely to catch up with their peers without early identification and intervention.

Data-driven decision making: RTI is rooted in using data to make decisions informing the reading instruction of each pupil. Universal screeners can help determine if a pupil is at risk for reading difficulties. If risk is determined, a further diagnostic assessment will be given to identify the skill deficit that will need to be targeted.

Fidelity of implementation: Evidence-based interventions should be implemented with fidelity and consistency. It is best practice for the instructor to keep a log of when the intervention took place and for how long. These details are important when assessing the effectiveness of the intervention.

Collaboration: It is essential for all stakeholders to be involved in the RTI process. Schools should foster open communication between teachers, parents, and all specialists involved in supporting a child's reading success.

Professional development: Educators and administrators should be provided with ongoing professional development on the Science of Reading. Coaching support will be crucial in helping educators see the work in action.

The RTI model, when aligned with the Science of Reading, offers a powerful process for addressing the diverse needs of learners. By integrating evidence-based practices, such as explicit instruction in foundational reading skills, RTI helps ensure that all pupils, particularly those struggling with reading, receive the timely and targeted support they need. Early identification, data-driven decision-making and tailored interventions are key to fostering literacy success. As schools continue to embrace the Science of Reading, RTI becomes an essential tool in creating equitable and effective learning environments where every pupil has the opportunity to thrive.

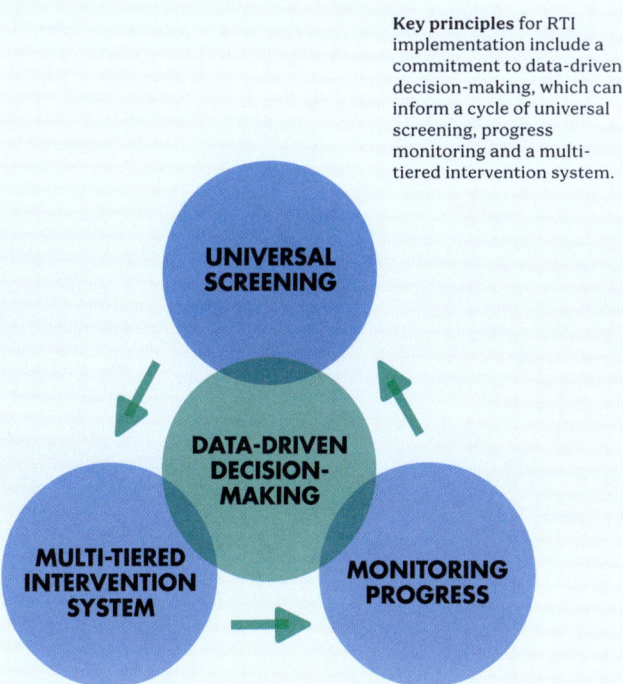

Key principles for RTI implementation include a commitment to data-driven decision-making, which can inform a cycle of universal screening, progress monitoring and a multi-tiered intervention system.

"Teachers can create a rich and engaging reading environment that fosters the development of lifelong readers."

Jake Downs

Empowering Learning Through Formative Assessments

by Alison Divino Driscoll

Formative assessments provide continuous feedback, helping teachers adjust instruction and supporting pupil learning. They encourage pupil involvement, promote self-reflection and improve outcomes.

What are formative assessments?

Formative assessments are powerful tools for gauging pupil mastery and understanding. They play a crucial role in instruction by providing continuous feedback throughout a module or unit, allowing teachers to adjust their instruction and support pupils in real time. These assessments not only enable teachers to monitor pupil progress, but they can also identify learning gaps and help teachers refine future instruction to meet pupils' needs. With formative assessments, there are no surprises. Their ongoing nature ensures that teachers and pupils are constantly aware of their progress toward mastery of the module or unit's goals.

When to implement formative assessments

Effective formative assessments align with the goals of the module or unit. This alignment ensures their impact, since the data from the assessments helps teachers adjust future lessons. These assessments may take place during a daily lesson and are particularly

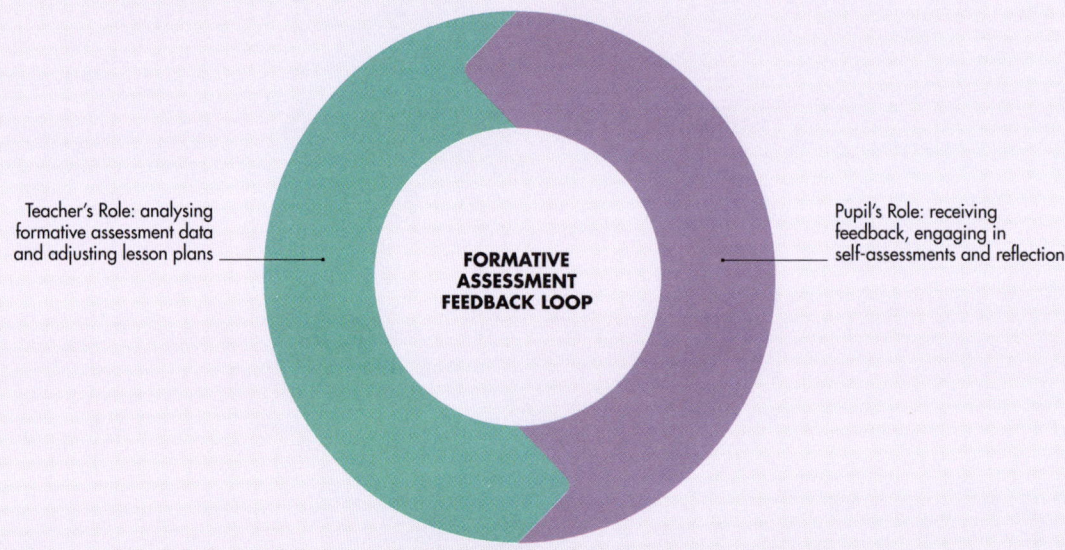

Teacher's Role: analysing formative assessment data and adjusting lesson plans

FORMATIVE ASSESSMENT FEEDBACK LOOP

Pupil's Role: receiving feedback, engaging in self-assessments and reflection

impactful because they are not treated as separate events, reducing the stress and anxiety that can often come with traditional test-taking. Formative assessments provide a cohesive learning experience for pupils, allowing them to feel safe and supported when demonstrating their knowledge.

Benefits of the formative assessment process

Teachers and pupils equally benefit from the use of formative assessments. Teachers can use the assessment data to modify and create more effective lessons, targeting areas where misunderstandings or gaps exist. Effective use and response to this data throughout a module or unit means that pupils are more likely to achieve the desired outcomes for the module or unit.

Pupils also benefit from formative assessments, but the instructional practices related to feedback and self-assessment should be more valued. Pupils benefit from using self-assessments or peer and teacher feedback to reflect on their strengths and identify areas for improvement. The data gives pupils agency in their learning experiences. Like teachers, pupils gain valuable insights that empower them to seek additional support or pursue extensions based on where they are.

How to implement formative assessments

Implementing formative assessments requires careful planning. Teachers must ensure that each assessment aligns with the learning goals and is appropriately placed within a sequence of instruction. Although the data is valuable, over-testing and abundant data can

overwhelm teachers and pupils. To ensure effectiveness and quality, teachers should pinpoint key moments of the sequence of instruction where a formative assessment would be valuable and provide data that would help identify gaps in understanding before the summative assessment. Additionally, assessments should be accessible and equitable, helping all pupils access, comprehend and demonstrate their knowledge.

Conclusion

Embedding formative assessments into instruction enables educators to create a supportive environment that enhances learning, fosters literacy development and encourages a culture of feedback and reflection. These assessments improve pupil outcomes and empower pupils to become lifelong learners who are actively engaged in their educational progress.

Three Tiers of Support for Pupils

The pyramid below, associated with both the response to intervention (RTI) and multi-tiered system of supports (MTSS) models, helps schools implement intervention strategies for pupils.

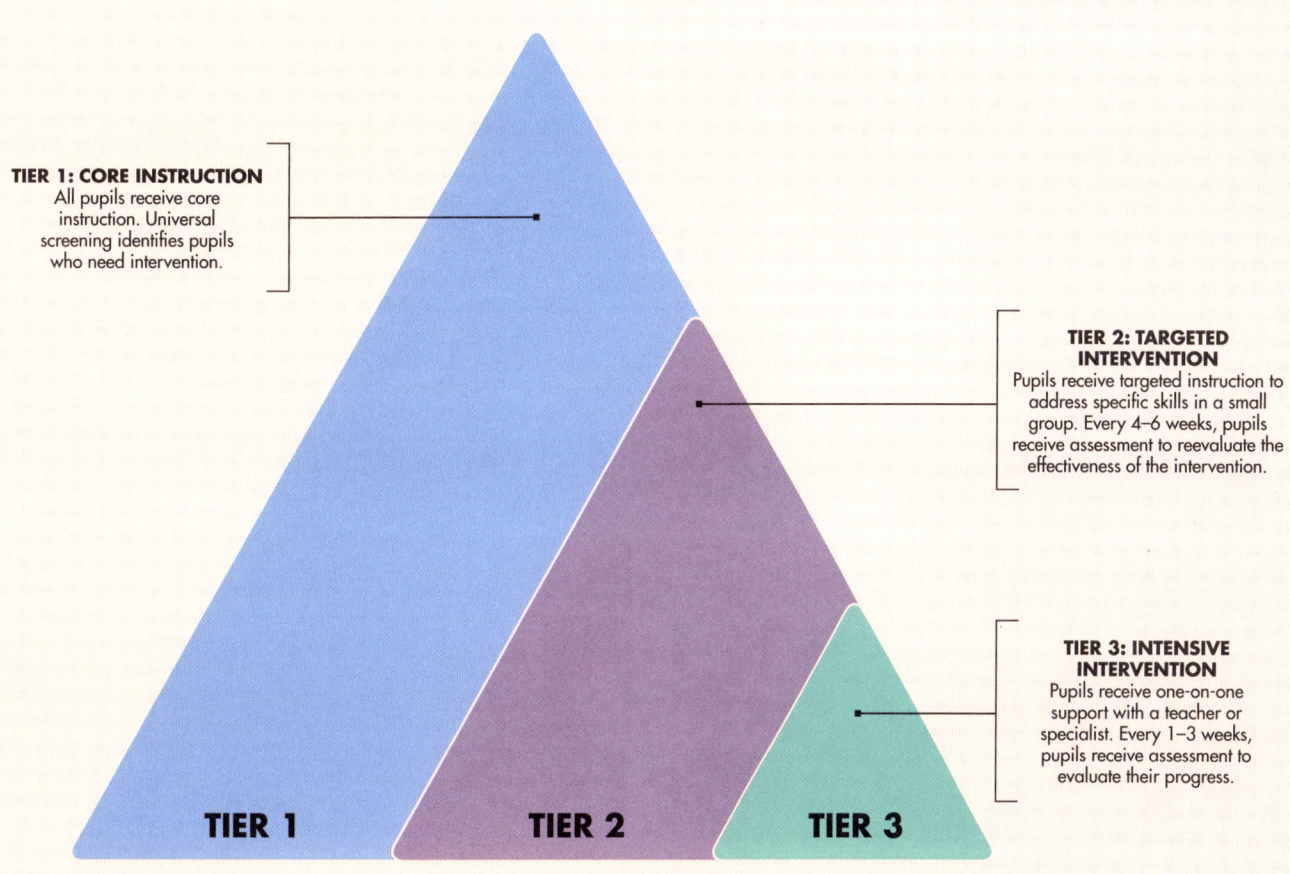

TIER 1: CORE INSTRUCTION
All pupils receive core instruction. Universal screening identifies pupils who need intervention.

TIER 2: TARGETED INTERVENTION
Pupils receive targeted instruction to address specific skills in a small group. Every 4–6 weeks, pupils receive assessment to reevaluate the effectiveness of the intervention.

TIER 3: INTENSIVE INTERVENTION
Pupils receive one-on-one support with a teacher or specialist. Every 1–3 weeks, pupils receive assessment to evaluate their progress.

ABOUT **80%** OF PUPILS WILL MASTER THE CONTENT FROM CORE CLASSROOM INSTRUCTION.

ABOUT **10-15%** OF PUPILS NEED TARGETED INTERVENTION IN A SMALL-GROUP SETTING.

ABOUT **5%** OR LESS OF PUPILS NEED INTENSIVE, INDIVIDUALISED INTERVENTION.

Using DIBELS for Diagnostic Assessment

by Laura Main

Diagnostic assessments are used to assess skills and pinpoint areas of weakness to target a focus for instruction. Dynamic Indicators of Basic Early Literacy Skills (DIBELS) is a diagnostic assessment focusing on foundational reading skills.

DIBELS is a valid and reliable measurement of early literacy skills that predict later reading achievement (University of Oregon, Center on Teaching and Learning, 2018–2020). The assessment is designed for pupils in grades K–8 (Reception through Year 9) in the US. DIBELS was developed and validated to effectively support individual pupils and pupil response to instruction, allowing teachers to identify pupils who are not on track for grade-level reading success (Kaminski & Cummings, 2007). The benchmark materials, scoring guide and progress monitoring materials are available for download at no cost at dibels.uoregon.edu/materials.

Subtests

Each DIBELS subtest is standardised and time-limited. The subtests and their difficulty are adjusted based on the pupil's grade level. Together, they assess letter recognition, phonemic awareness, phonics skills, word reading, fluency and comprehension.

Phonemic Awareness is the ability to hear and manipulate sounds in spoken words, and it predicts future reading success. The Phonemic Segmentation Fluency (PSF) subtest is administered in grades K and 1 (Year 1 and 2).

Phonics is the ability to learn individual sounds and to map them to specific written letters. Pupils with strong skills in this area can connect individual sounds to letters to read words. Two subtests measure phonics and are administered in grades K–3 (Years 1–4). The Nonsense Word Fluency-Correct Letter Sounds (NWF-CLS) subtest measures basic phonics skills. The Nonsense Word Fluency-Words Recorded Correctly (NWF-WRC) subtest measures basic phonics skills and blending.

Fluency is the ability to read text accurately with automaticity. Two subtests measure fluency and are administered in grades 1–8 (Years 2–9). The Oral Reading Fluency-Words Correct (ORF-WC) subtest measures the ability to read words accurately and automatically. The Oral Reading Fluency-Accuracy (ORF-Accuracy) subtest measures the percentage of words the pupil reads correctly in a passage.

Comprehension is understanding what has been read, which is the ultimate goal of reading instruction. The MAZE subtest measures reading comprehension and is administered in grades 2–8 (Years 3–9).

> **Progress monitoring**
> Subtests provide opportunities to evaluate progress with specific skills.

DIBELS subtests by grade level

TYPE	GRADES ASSESSED					
	K	1	2	3	4-6	7-8
First Sound Fluency (FSF) or Initial Sound Fluency (ISF)	✓					
Phoneme Segmentation Fluency (PSF)	✓	✓				
Letter Naming Fluency	✓	✓				
Nonsense Word Fluency (NWF)	✓	✓	✓	✓		
Word Reading Fluency (WRF)	✓	✓	✓	✓		
Oral Reading Fluency (ORF)		✓	✓	✓	✓	✓
MAZE			✓	✓	✓	✓
DAZE				✓	✓	

Test of related early literacy skills

A separate but related subtest is administered in grades K and 1. The Letter Naming Fluency (LNF) subtest measures the pupil's ability to name upper and lowercase letters of the alphabet, which is a strong predictor of future reading success.

Universal screening and progress monitoring

DIBELS can be used for universal screening of all pupils in grades K–8 (Years 2–9) three times a year. It has also been validated as a dyslexia screener (Ives et al., 2019).

Once an instructional focus is selected and instruction has been given with fidelity for at least two weeks, the DIBELS subtests can be used to measure a pupil's response to intervention. Other screeners may be needed to make additional instructional decisions to fine-tune a pupil's instructional needs.

When administering the DIBELS benchmark or progress monitoring tools, follow the standardised testing procedures. Once testing is complete, teachers may develop an intervention plan for each pupil and create flexible groups for small-group instruction.

DIBELS is not intended to be used as the sole measure of pupil success but instead within a system of literacy support used to support data-based decision-making (Kaminski & Cummings, 2007). Using a single indicator for decision-making violates the professional standards of measurement (American Educational Research Association et al., 1999).

DID THE PUPIL PERFORM PROFICIENTLY DURING THE SCREENING?

Yes

The pupil should achieve their reading goals using core instruction.

No

Use intervention to provide additional support and progress monitoring to assess pupils' skills.

Evaluating Reading Through Summative Assessment

by Ashley Carrigan, Georgette Morgan and Denise Ross

Summative assessments are pivotal in determining whether pupils have achieved a set of learning outcomes. They provide actionable insights into pupil performance, guiding interventions and instructional adjustments to attain long-term success.

Summative assessments evaluate reading proficiency after instruction, such as at the end of a term or school year. Results summarise a pupil's performance and can help educators make informed decisions to improve reading outcomes. Unlike formative assessments, which measure progress during instruction, summative assessments evaluate overall mastery of learning outcomes at the conclusion of a unit, course or period of time.

These assessments can be used to measure a number of different reading-related repertoires including phonemic awareness, phonics, vocabulary, comprehension and writing, among others. Summative assessments can include standardised reading assessments (e.g., national reading tests); criterion-referenced tests (e.g., curriculum-based assessments) or norm-referenced tests that compare pupils to others of a similar age or year group. These tests are typically administered at different points in the year such as the beginning and end of a term, course or school year. They are called summative assessments because results are used to summarise a pupil's progress. Results also inform instructional planning, highlight areas that need additional intervention and measure pupils' attainment of established reading benchmarks.

Selecting and administering summative assessments

When selecting and developing summative assessments in reading, it is important to first identify the purpose of the assessment. For example, is the assessment intended to inform instruction, identify the need for intervention or aid in broader educational decisions such as if a pupil should be further evaluated for

reading disabilities? After determining the purpose of a summative reading assessment, teachers ensure that it is aligned with instruction or benchmarks that pupils were expected to attain during a specified time period. It is also important to select tests that are both reliable and valid, which means that they repeatedly produce consistent outcomes and measure what they are intended to measure. In reading, it is important to ensure that summative assessments are sensitive to the different repertoires and backgrounds that pupils may have. For instance, some tests are better for pupils with reading disabilities when compared to other tests. Finally, when administering summative assessments, it is important to follow all guidelines for giving the test to ensure that results can be accurately interpreted.

Making summative assessments effective

To maximise the effectiveness of summative assessments, educators should integrate them into instruction alongside formative and diagnostic assessments. Summative assessments, such as those from the previous year, provide baseline data to guide individualised instruction and compare performance to benchmarks. Teachers can then use diagnostic assessments to identify specific reading needs and formative assessments during instruction to adjust teaching strategies, such as tracking phonics mastery and fluency. At the end of a unit or term, summative assessments evaluate whether pupils meet benchmarks, ensuring a comprehensive approach to monitoring progress and planning instruction.

The value and criticisms of summative assessments

While summative assessments cannot capture the daily nuances of learning, they remain vital for summarising pupils' achievements and identifying areas for growth. Combined with formative assessments and observational data, summative assessments create a holistic approach to fostering literacy development. However, while summative assessments are helpful, they can be challenging for pupils when used as high-stakes assessments. High-stakes assessments are assessments that are tied to consequences for pupils such as requiring them to repeat a year if they are not reading at, or near, the expected standard for their year group. Relatedly, norm-referenced assessments have been criticised when their normative samples do not include pupils from multiple backgrounds. It is important, therefore, for teachers to maximise the effectiveness of summative assessment by integrating them seamlessly into the instructional process, balancing them with formative and diagnostic assessments.

Benchmark assessments
Monitor pupils' progress and serve as a point of reference.

Instructional Strategies and Equity in Literacy

Scaffolding: A Key to Supporting All Pupils — 136

Think-Aloud Strategies — 139

Think-Alouds: Modelling Reading as Thinking — 140

The Science of Reading and Cultural Understanding — 142

Equity and Literacy — 144

Family Contribution to the Development of Skilled Readers — 149

Cooperative Learning — 154

Strengthening Literacy Through Collaboration — 157

Small-Group Reading Instruction — 160

The Gradual Release of Responsibility: Transforming Literacy Instruction — 162

The Power of Explicit Instruction in Literacy — 166

Defining Dyslexia — 169

Supporting Pupils with Dyslexia in the Classroom — 172

Drawn to the Code: Hyperlexia and Reading — 176

Specific Reading Comprehension Deficit — 178

Scaffolding: A Key to Supporting All Pupils

by Alison Divino Driscoll

Scaffolding is a vital instructional strategy that supports all pupils mastering year-group material. Educators can enhance learning, promote engagement and ensure academic equity by providing targeted input and output scaffolds.

Meeting pupils where they are is essential, but assigning work below year-group expectations can hinder their progress. Excellent teachers ensure all pupils can access year-group material and receive support. Scaffolding is a key tool for achieving this goal, as it allows teachers to maintain high expectations without lowering standards.

Effective scaffolding is explicit and used strategically. Scaffolds build efficiency and competence by breaking down the components of a complex skill and embedding supports that allow pupils to comprehend the new learning or demonstrate their understanding. Over time, teachers use fewer scaffolds as pupils develop fluency, accuracy and familiarity with the practised skills. The ultimate goal of scaffolding is to eliminate unnecessary complexities during the learning process and help pupils apply new skills confidently and independently.

> "Effective scaffolding is explicit and used strategically."

The big idea: Narrowing the scope

Scaffolding aims to narrow the scope, guide pupils' attention to key components, and provide targeted support. Scaffolding strategies fall into two categories:

Input scaffolds help pupils process new information through tools like focused annotations, visual aids, and breaking complex ideas into manageable parts.

Output scaffolds enable pupils to demonstrate understanding using sentence stems, graphic organisers and word banks.

Input and output scaffolds ensure pupils can engage fully in learning by bridging gaps in comprehension or demonstration, making them accessible without sacrificing rigour.

INPUT SCAFFOLDS
Text annotations
Visual aids
Breaking down complex ideas

OUTPUT SCAFFOLDS
Sentence stems
Graphic organisers
Word banks

Practical lesson planning

Effective scaffolding begins with clearly understanding pupils' needs and lesson objectives.

Teachers can use data gathered from ongoing assessments to identify barriers to pupils' access to the skill taught.

To scaffold effectively, teachers must understand their pupils, including:

- **Who is in their class, and where are they academically?**
- **What are the expectations for their work?**
- **Why do these expectations differ? (if applicable)**

This knowledge enables teachers to tailor instruction to meet pupils' needs while maintaining the necessary rigor for the task or skill.

Although scaffolding is necessary for complex tasks or skills, teachers should ensure scaffolds align with learning objectives. Using too many scaffolds in a lesson could lead to a less engaging and rigorous experience for pupils. To ensure lessons remain engaging, teachers should reflect on the learning objectives and identify scaffolds that closely align with the existing barriers so that pupils can effectively climb the "ladder" of skills necessary to master the objectives.

This reflective process ensures scaffolds remain effective, responsive to pupils' needs and aligned with instructional goals.

Conclusion

Scaffolding bridges the gap between where pupils are and where they need to be, supporting learning at every stage. Educators can ensure that pupils can comprehend and demonstrate year-group skills by using data to understand what barriers exist for their pupils, balancing input and output scaffolds, and aligning scaffolds to lesson objectives. Scaffolding enhances instruction and promotes equity, empowering learners to master essential skills. With thoughtful planning, implementation and reflection, scaffolding becomes a transformative tool for academic success.

Think-Aloud Strategies
by Elizabeth K. Waller

Educators can use think-alouds to show how expert readers monitor their thinking and make connections as they read. Use think-alouds to monitor strategies for reading and rereading to improve comprehension of a text.

THINK-ALOUD STRATEGY	PURPOSE	SENTENCE STARTERS
PREDICT	Use clues from the title, text and illustrations or graphics to predict or infer what will happen.	I predict… In the next part, I think…
CONNECT	Use background knowledge to connect what you read to what you already know.	This reminds me of… This is like… This makes me think of…
EVALUATE	Form opinions about the text as you read.	I enjoyed… One thing I liked was…
VISUALISE	Use mental images to help you picture the events and characters in the text.	I can picture…
IDENTIFY	Recognise text structures and features.	I think the author is comparing and contrasting…
QUESTION	Identify areas of confusion and ask yourself questions to see if the text makes sense.	I'm wondering about… I need to look back and reread… I was confused about…

Think-Alouds: Modelling Reading as Thinking

by Elizabeth K. Waller

The use of the think-aloud strategy helps pupils connect to new knowledge by encouraging them to periodically stop reading to verbalise their thinking about what they have read and what they anticipate they will read.

The think-aloud strategy is an interactive meta-cognitive reading comprehension strategy that has been around since the 1970s. Think-alouds help pupils build reading comprehension by learning thought processes that help them ask questions, reflect on what they have read, adjust their reading pace and employ other thought processes that skilled readers use to connect what they read to what they already know.

Thinking about reading

Skilled readers use specific thought processes before, during and after reading. Essentially, they are active readers who monitor their comprehension. Below average and struggling readers struggle with reading words without thinking about the meanings. They are inactive readers.

The think-aloud strategy

Pupils learn to make connections between what they read/hear and what they already know. Pupils learn to employ these strategies as they read:

- draw on background knowledge
- make predictions
- visualise the events of a text
- recognise confusion
- recognise a text's structure/organisation
- identify/recognise a purpose for reading
- visualise the events of a text
  (Farr & Connor, 2015)

Teachers must carefully plan and implement effective think-aloud activities. The teacher must put together a plan to manage the discussions that need to take place for pupils to engage in meaningful dialogues with the teacher and their peers about what they are reading.

The teacher selects a long reading passage or book and demonstrates how an expert reader thinks as they read. The teacher will stop reading periodically to ask questions, make predictions, reread sections and summarise the readings to model what thought processes need to happen when the pupils read. Think-alouds help pupils discover what questions, thoughts, connections, reflections and predictions they need to emulate to become skilled readers.

Think-alouds for assessment

The teacher models and demonstrates these processes over several sessions. Reading daily from a chapter book, such as *Charlotte's Web*, provides multiple opportunities for the teacher to coach pupils, as they begin independently using the prompts learned in discussions about the daily read-aloud. As teachers listen in on what pupils are verbalising when they think aloud, they can gain insights into how pupils apply the processes they are learning.

Think-aloud skills are transferable

When pupils become comfortable with the strategy of think-alouds, they can easily begin to apply the thinking processes they have learned to other learning tasks. They can ask many of the same questions to help solve problems in mathematics, science, social studies, music and art.

Special education pupils and multilingual learners can gain confidence by learning think-aloud strategies. The think-aloud processes are as useful for building independent thinking skills for diverse populations as they are for struggling readers. Parents who want to support their children's learning can also use think-aloud strategy questions at home when they read to their children. There seems to be no limit to the benefits of using think-alouds inside or outside of reading instruction or the classroom.

The Science of Reading and Cultural Understanding

by Keshiea Chandler

Understanding how cultural experiences shape literacy development helps educators and parents support children in becoming confident readers while honouring their diverse backgrounds and experiences.

Culturally responsive literacy begins with recognising and valuing the rich knowledge and experiences children bring from their homes and communities into the classroom. These cultural assets encompass more than just language variations; they include unique storytelling traditions passed down through generations, diverse communication styles that reflect family and community values and varied literacy experiences that may differ from traditional school-based practices. When educators acknowledge and build upon these cultural foundations, they transform potential challenges into powerful opportunities for literacy development.

Research-based impact on reading success

Research consistently demonstrates the profound impact of cultural connection on literacy success. When pupils encounter texts and learning experiences that mirror their cultural backgrounds, they show not only increased engagement but also demonstrate deeper text comprehension and make more meaningful connections to reading material. A pupil who sees their family traditions, community experiences or cultural celebrations reflected in classroom texts is more likely to activate their background knowledge, a key component emphasised by the Science of Reading.

Integrating culturally responsive literacy with the Science of Reading

The integration of cultural responsiveness with Science of Reading principles can take many practical forms. When teaching phonological awareness, educators might incorporate multilingual nursery rhymes, cultural songs or familiar community chants that pupils know from home. For instance, Spanish-speaking pupils might work with syllable awareness through traditional *canciones*, while pupils from oral storytelling traditions might explore rhythm and rhyme through familiar narrative patterns. This approach simultaneously develops crucial phonological skills while affirming pupils' cultural identities. In vocabulary instruction, new words gain deeper meaning when connected to pupils'

"Parents and caregivers are essential partners in culturally responsive literacy development."

Ways to incorporate culturally responsive literacy in your classroom

INCORPORATE SONGS AND RHYMES FROM DIFFERENT CULTURES

CHOOSE MATERIALS BY AUTHORS FROM VARIED CULTURAL BACKGROUNDS

PROVIDE MULTIPLE PATHWAYS FOR PUPILS TO DEMONSTRATE THEIR READING COMPREHENSION

lived experiences – for example, teaching words like *perseverance* through stories of family immigration, or *community* through examples from pupils' neighbourhoods.

Selecting culturally authentic texts

Text selection requires thoughtful consideration of both academic rigour and cultural authenticity. While maintaining appropriate text complexity levels, educators should seek out materials that genuinely represent diverse perspectives and experiences. This means moving beyond surface-level diversity to include texts written by authors from varied cultural backgrounds, featuring authentic character experiences and addressing real-world themes that resonate with pupils' lives.

Assessment and cultural awareness

Assessment practices in culturally responsive literacy must balance scientific rigour with cultural awareness. While measuring essential reading skills remains crucial, educators should consider how cultural experiences might influence pupil responses. This might involve providing multiple ways for pupils to demonstrate their understanding or considering cultural communication patterns when assessing oral reading fluency.

Home-school partnership

Parents and caregivers are essential partners in culturally responsive literacy development. They can share valuable insights about their children's cultural backgrounds, helping educators build meaningful connections between home and school literacy practices. This partnership strengthens the implementation of Science of Reading principles by ensuring that instruction resonates with pupils' lived experiences.

PUPILS WHO READ CULTURALLY RELEVANT TEXTS ARE **16%** MORE LIKELY TO MAKE CONNECTIONS TO THE TEXTS.

HOWEVER, ONLY ABOUT **15%** OF CHILDREN'S BOOKS FEATURE BLACK OR LATINO CHARACTERS.

Equity and Literacy

by Kareem J. Weaver

Literacy is a fundamental right that drives equity in education. By setting high expectations, improving teaching quality and fostering supportive leadership, pupils can be empowered, thrive and succeed.

All pupils can learn. This belief is foundational to ensuring every child has the opportunity and support needed to become fully literate. It compels us to critically examine educational systems and their outcomes. It demands ongoing, comprehensive evaluation of teacher preparation, leadership teams, instructional materials and school environments. And it ensures personal biases do not cloud the expectations we set for our pupils.

> "There is no equity without literacy."

True equity requires confronting the gap between our ideals and the academic realities many pupils face. For those bold enough to wrestle with these instructional and institutional challenges, change is possible; managing it, however, often requires uncomfortable shifts.

Much like the Statue of Liberty, whose torch symbolises freedom but whose feet are bound by chains, the full promise of liberty remains inaccessible without the skill to read. Illiteracy is a form of bondage, holding people in place and preventing them from moving forward in life. True commitment to equity means first breaking the organisational and pedagogical chains that consign children, especially those in high-needs communities, to the margins of society.

Literacy as a fundamental right

Literacy is not just a skill but a fundamental human and civil right, crucial for societal participation and personal development. It is a moral imperative that reflects our societal values of fairness and justice. Organisations like the NAACP and the Ontario Human Rights Commission recognise literacy as pivotal in achieving social equity. There is no equity without literacy. Here are the key ingredients that must be addressed to secure it.

Unlike equality, which treats everyone the same, equity considers differences to eliminate barriers, reduce disparities and promote inclusion.

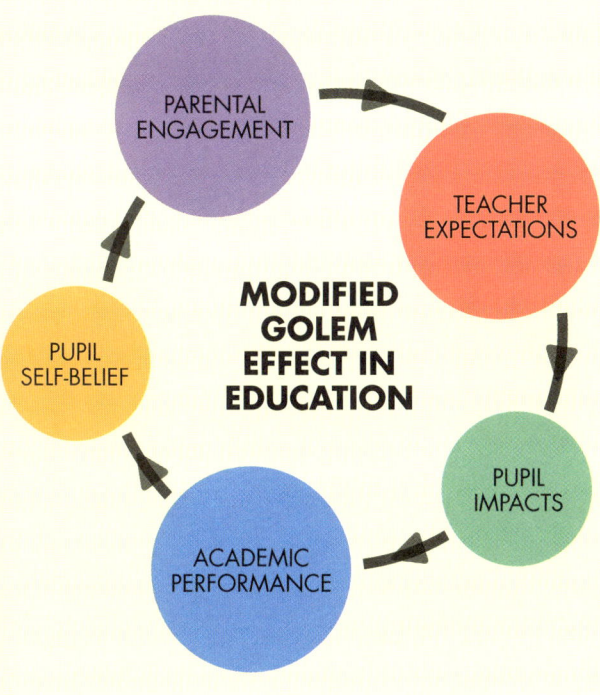

The Golem Effect is a psychological phenomenon in which low expectations from superiors such as teachers lead to poorer performance. Pupils' negative beliefs about themselves directly hinder their achievement.

Combatting low expectations

Every pupil deserves high expectations. Failure to consistently maintain a standard of excellence significantly limits educational attainment and stifles potential. This issue is compounded by the Discrepancy Model, which looks at "expected performance" and identifies individuals who need additional support based on the degree to which they deviate from that expectation. When educators rely on this model without having high expectations, they risk invoking the Golem effect, where low expectations lead to diminished performance and reduced motivation. This undermines effective instruction, identifying gaps in learning and providing timely interventions. Proactively setting high expectations, coupled with strong support systems, enables pupils to achieve their fullest potential and dismantle long-standing educational barriers.

High-quality teaching

Instructional quality is a crucial element of pupil literacy success. Effective training, grounded in the Science of Reading, provides educators with the essential skills needed for comprehensive literacy development. This perspective is supported by the 2007 McKinsey Report, which states, "The caliber of an education system cannot exceed the quality of its teaching." Therefore, ongoing professional development, tailored to the latest educational research, is critical to equip regular, hardworking teachers with the strategies necessary for consistent success. By ensuring that all educators receive this support, we set up our pupils for sustained high achievement in literacy.

Proven materials

Instructional materials are not proven unless they demonstrate—through rigorous evidence—the ability to reliably enhance pupil achievement. Such materials need to align closely with academic standards and be tested in diverse classroom settings to ensure they effectively support all pupils in mastering complex texts. The goal is to provide curricula that not only meet but *exceed* the requirements for comprehensive literacy education, thereby narrowing the achievement gap.

APPROXIMATELY **654 MILLION** ADULTS LACK BASIC LITERACY SKILLS WORLDWIDE.

ONE-THIRD OF ADULTS WITH LOW LITERACY ARE UNEMPLOYED IN THE US.

THE GLOBAL ECONOMIC COST OF ILLITERACY IS APPROXIMATELY **$1.19 TRILLION** ANNUALLY.

CHILDREN OF COLOUR ARE DISPROPORTIONATELY AFFECTED BY EDUCATIONAL DISPARITIES.

Planning time: Essential for tailoring education

Effective planning blocks are crucial for educators to adapt proven curricula to the specific needs of their pupils. This dedicated time allows teachers to identify and bridge gaps in both the curriculum and pupils' understanding, infusing the content with relevance and vigour. Good educators know that planning is where the magic of teaching begins. This underscores the significance of protected time for planning, which is vital for realising the potential to close literacy gaps and genuinely engage pupils.

Leadership and school culture: Catalysts for change

True leadership extends beyond routine administrative tasks; it involves building a culture that champions literacy and quality instruction. Leaders committed to educational equity have the power to transform schools into vibrant environments where high educational standards are the norm. Through building consensus, fostering collaboration and spearheading strategic initiatives, they ensure the school's culture and operational strategies align with educational equity goals.

Skilled leadership identifies and supports the technical aspects of an effective literacy programme. It attends to the science of learning and ensures there are high-functioning systems in place that support teaching and learning. But change is personal. Human beings need support managing the change process, and it is the leaders' responsibility to provide support across a range of levers, described aptly by the Lippitt–Knoster Model of Change. Bureaucratic efficiencies alone, will not yield the universal access to excellence – the equity – that all children deserve. There must be a clear vision, consensus secured, skills developed, resources provided and an action plan that is created, implemented and monitored.

Cultural foundations for empowering growth

Effective reading programmes can only succeed in a culture that supports continuous learning and improvement. This nurturing environment is critical for empowering educators to explore and refine new teaching strategies with confidence, thus supporting the successful implementation of evidence-based literacy practices.

Empowering growth through collective efficacy

Creating and maintaining a mindset that prioritises growth alongside collective teacher efficacy profoundly influences literacy achievement. When teachers believe in their collective capacity to enhance pupil outcomes and are supported by a culture that values growth, they achieve remarkable literacy gains. This empowerment is essential for fostering an educational atmosphere where challenges are seen as opportunities for development and success.

> **Collective efficacy**
> Educators can foster pupil growth when they share a belief in their ability to positively impact pupil outcomes.

Lippitt–Knoster Model for Managing Complex Change

The Lippitt–Knoster Model for Managing Complex Change is a framework designed to facilitate effective change management. Developed by Lippitt and Knoster, the model emphasises the interplay of several critical components that must be present for successful change initiatives: vision, consensus, skills, incentives, resources and an action plan.

VISION	CONSENSUS	SKILLS	INCENTIVES	RESOURCES	ACTION PLAN	→	SUCCESS
VISION	CONSENSUS	SKILLS	INCENTIVES	RESOURCES	ACTION PLAN	→	CONFUSION
VISION	CONSENSUS	SKILLS	INCENTIVES	RESOURCES	ACTION PLAN	→	SABOTAGE
VISION	CONSENSUS	SKILLS	INCENTIVES	RESOURCES	ACTION PLAN	→	ANXIETY
VISION	CONSENSUS	SKILLS	INCENTIVES	RESOURCES	ACTION PLAN	→	RESISTANCE
VISION	CONSENSUS	SKILLS	INCENTIVES	RESOURCES	ACTION PLAN	→	FRUSTRATION
VISION	CONSENSUS	SKILLS	INCENTIVES	RESOURCES	ACTION PLAN	→	FALSE STARTS

> **"Without literacy, people are left on the margins, unable to fully participate in civic life or make informed decisions."**

Conclusion: A unified call to action

Achieving universal literacy is not merely an educational challenge; it is a societal imperative that requires operationalised equity. Literacy is the bedrock of modern society and the fulcrum by which our rights and duties are balanced. Without literacy, people are left on the margins, unable to fully participate in civic life or make informed decisions that impact their health, well-being and future. Whether it's reading a ballot, understanding a legal document or interpreting health information, literacy grants individuals the power to access vital institutions and resources. It is the cornerstone for true autonomy.

When we equip every child with the ability to read, we reduce inequities, create pathways out of poverty and build stronger, more informed communities. Literate individuals are more likely to access higher education, secure well-paying jobs and actively participate in civic duties. In turn, this contributes to a more just, prosperous and cohesive society.

To make this a reality, our educational institutions must ensure access to well-prepared teachers, adopt curricula and methods proven to be effective, and provide educators with the time and resources they need to fully implement these practices. By dismantling barriers to literacy and building systems that reflect our commitment to both equity and excellence, we empower every child to thrive in a complex and interconnected world. This is not simply an educational goal – it is the key to unlocking the potential within each individual and the foundation upon which a more equitable and just society can be built.

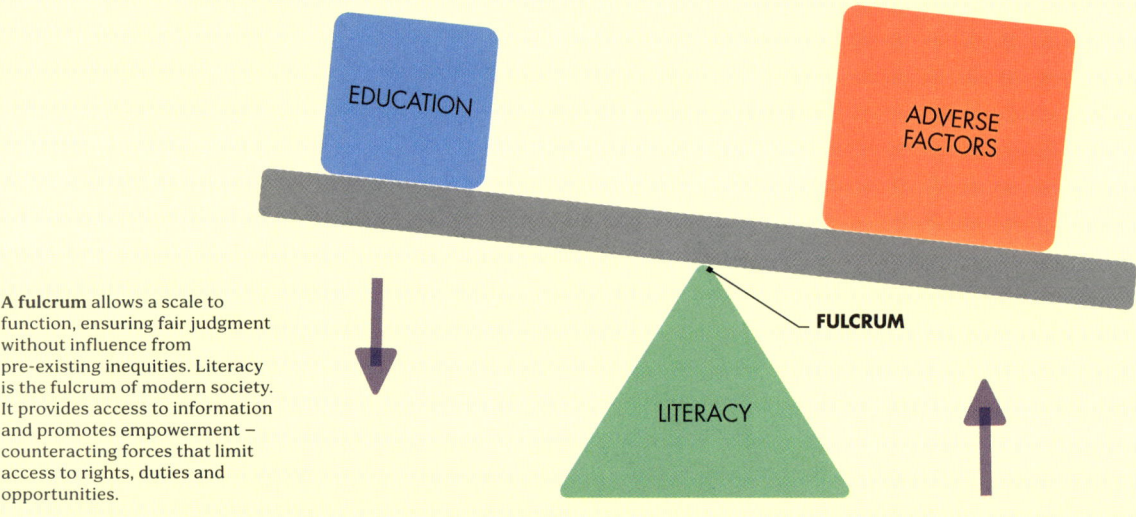

A fulcrum allows a scale to function, ensuring fair judgment without influence from pre-existing inequities. Literacy is the fulcrum of modern society. It provides access to information and promotes empowerment – counteracting forces that limit access to rights, duties and opportunities.

Family Contribution to the Development of Skilled Readers

by Jessica Page Bergeron

Families and caregivers play a crucial role in children's early literacy by providing a strong foundation in language.

The most important contribution families and caregivers can make to their child's outcomes in reading is to promote oral language in the home from birth through age five before formal reading instruction begins. Two very robust strategies to promote oral language during this time are sharing conversations (i.e., narrating your day, asking questions, etc.) and interactive shared reading.

While the Science of Reading has given educators a road map for reading instruction, if pupils are without a solid foundation in oral language, they are at a measurable disadvantage compared to their peers. The disadvantage not only has an impact on reading comprehension when children make the transition from learning to read to reading to learn, but also appears when learning decoding and phonemic awareness skills. While very young children may not be skilled in verbalising much of what they hear and understand, these early years build the foundation for positive literacy outcomes later on, particularly for reading comprehension and expressing themselves in writing.

What do we know about oral language contributions to literacy?

Literacy is a language activity. Listening and talking in almost any language can be encoded into reading and writing. When young children begin formal reading instruction, the instruction is focused on the mechanics of reading rather than on language and vocabulary instruction. For children with proficient language skills, the instruction on the mechanics of reading involves connecting an already robust language system that has been developed from their environment from birth to age five. Word decoding leads to understanding (comprehension) because the meaning of the word is already well established in their memory.

Without a strong foundation in language, children cannot adequately comprehend words, decode new words or learn new meaning from

Family–School Partnerships

CAREGIVERS CAN SET CHILDREN UP FOR SUCCESS WITH READING FROM EARLY CHILDHOOD.
As children start and continue with school, family contributions continue to be essential. Routines involving shared reading help children become proficient readers.

> "Parents who read books and share conversations with their children develop language-rich environments."

the text. That means the effect of a language deficit on reading achievement may not be observable until after Year 3 when instruction shifts from the mechanics of reading (learning to read) to comprehension and learning from the text (reading to learn). In fact, language is a stronger predictor of reading achievement in Year 5 than in Year 2. It would be more effective to provide robust language experiences so that children can begin reading instruction with the best possible foundation for success.

How can parents create a language-rich environment?

Interactive shared reading—when parents have a conversation around the book with their child, rather than just reading the text to their child—has a plethora of research to support positive effects on language development and as a predictor for reading achievement. It contributes to literacy in several areas beyond language development, including print concepts such as alphabetic knowledge, phonological awareness, early reading and writing, and even spelling. Shared reading can also mediate delays in language for children who may be at risk for language delays due to lack of access or exposure and/or the presence of disabilities. Parents can set up a nightly bedtime or playtime routine that includes books or conversation using conversational strategies.

Building oral language does not require specialised instruction or additional formal education to implement effectively. Parents who read books and share conversations with their children develop language-rich environments, which lead to positive outcomes in oral language necessary to become a proficient reader.

INSTRUCTIONAL STRATEGIES AND EQUITY IN LITERACY 151

CONVERSATIONAL TECHNIQUE	DESCRIPTION/EXAMPLES
REVISIT THE BOOK OR IDEAS FROM THE BOOK.	"I remember the duck in the book said 'quack.'" "Let's reread the same book from last night about the duck." "Oooh, I see a duck! That's like the one from the book." "Let's feed some ducks at the park."
ASK OPEN-ENDED QUESTIONS.	Ask *wh-* questions: "Where will he go?" "What is that?
ENCOURAGE YOUR CHILD TO TALK ABOUT THE STORY OR RETELL THE STORY.	Ask your child to tell you about the story or what happened in the story. Use fill-in-the-blank sentences: "He fed the ducks at _____."
EXPAND YOUR CHILD'S LANGUAGE.	Repeat back what your child said and add one or two words.

"**Pupils who work together are learning more than just academics. They are also learning how to interact and share in the joy of learning.**"

Elizabeth K. Waller

Cooperative Learning

by Elizabeth K. Waller

In an educational landscape where competition has been the norm, cooperative learning is helping pupils learn how to communicate with their peers and work toward common academic goals.

Pupils who are encouraged to work together in pairs, groups and noncompetitive teams are learning more than just academics. They are also learning how to interact, cooperate, and share in the joy of learning.

What is cooperative learning?

Cooperative learning is more than group work. Yes, it is pupils working in groups, but these groups are comprised of pupils of mixed abilities. These heterogeneous groups allow pupils to learn different ways of thinking. The more diverse the groups, the more pupils learn from one another. For example, people may think that just because some pupils can't read, they can't think. On the contrary, pupils who struggle with reading may have any number of issues that make reading difficult, and yet they can learn and share their thinking via other modalities. The goal of cooperative learning is to take the competitiveness out of pupil interactions.

Key elements of cooperative learning

In addition to the mixed ability grouping, cooperative learning differs from ordinary group work in several other respects. Cooperative learning elements include the following:

- Face-to-face interaction
- Positive interdependence
- Individual accountability
- Group processing
- Collaborative skills
  (Johnson & Johnson, 1994)

Teachers must carefully teach all of these elements so that the group members understand that while the group is accountable for achieving its goals, the group's success is dependent on each group member's success as well.

Teaching the key elements

The teacher can model all of these elements. However, activating pupil engagement will probably have the most impact. Role-playing and discussion in simulated scenarios are ways for pupils to practise active listening, compromise and conflict resolution.

These activities cover at least three of the key elements: face-to-face interactions, group processing and collaborative skills.

Assigning tasks where each group member has information that the others need to complete the task, and setting shared goals for the group will lead the pupils to learn to focus on positive interdependence. They will have to rely on each other to complete the task as a group, successfully.

To ensure individual (and group) accountability, the teacher can

- question any pupil in a group on the material in the task
- have every pupil in the group write about the material
- observe pupils as they verbally interact and rehearse the information

Strategies used in cooperative learning classrooms

Some of these strategies are already familiar to teachers. However, when they focus on implementing the key elements of cooperative learning, these strategies will garner higher achievement levels.

In a think-pair-share, individual learners think about a question and develop ideas in response to the question. Then, they pair with another learner and share their ideas.

In a jigsaw activity, each group member has information that the others need to complete the task. That group member is responsible for learning that part of the topic and teaching it to the group members.

Teachers can use group projects, assigning work to complete over a full class period or an extended period of time. They also can assign roles for each pupil in the group.

In peer tutoring, pupils work in pairs or small groups with one pupil being the tutor to help another pupil or pupils learn a concept. These are just a few strategies that teachers may currently use as group work that can easily translate to cooperative group work by introducing cooperative learning's key elements.

The most important things to remember in a cooperative learning classroom are that group size should be flexible depending on the goal of the activity, the groups should be heterogeneous, learning in a non-competitive environment allows for greater achievement and teachers are still the maestros who make it all work.

Think-pair-share

THINK
Each pupil thinks in response to a question or problem.

PAIR
Pupils talk about their responses with partners.

SHARE
Each pair of pupils shares their thoughts with the class.

Jigsaw activity

STAGE 1 – FOCUS OR EXPERT GROUPS
Pupils work in groups of three to five.
Assign each group a text or topic to discuss.

STAGE 2 – MIXED GROUPS
Pupils share the knowledge they learned in a mixed group.
They may apply what they learned to discuss a task or question.

Strengthening Literacy Through Collaboration

by Keshiea Chandler

Grounded in the Science of Reading, cooperative learning ensures that pupils not only build foundational reading skills but also develop comprehension, critical thinking and communication through structured, interactive learning experiences.

The Science of Reading emphasises systematic instruction in phonemic awareness, phonics, fluency, vocabulary and comprehension. Cooperative learning supports these components by creating a social and interactive environment where pupils learn with and from one another.

The role of cooperative learning in literacy development

When structured effectively, cooperative learning enables pupils to practise literacy skills in meaningful contexts, reinforcing their ability to decode, interpret and analyse texts. It is an instructional approach that enhances literacy development by fostering peer collaboration and active engagement.

One of the key benefits of cooperative learning is that it allows pupils to engage in discussion-based reading activities, encouraging them to articulate their thoughts, question texts and clarify their understanding. This form of active learning is particularly beneficial for struggling readers, as it provides multiple opportunities for guided practice, immediate feedback and reinforcement of reading strategies.

Strategies for implementing cooperative learning in literacy instruction

Implementing cooperative learning in literacy instruction transforms the traditional classroom into an interactive learning environment where pupils actively support each other's growth. At the heart of this approach lies partner reading and peer-assisted learning, where pupils work in pairs to develop their reading skills. During these sessions, pupils take it in turns reading aloud while their partners provide constructive feedback, creating a supportive atmosphere that naturally enhances fluency and comprehension.

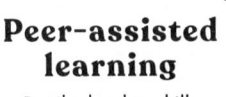

Peer-assisted learning
Pupils develop skills through offering each other feedback.

This collaborative spirit extends into literature circles, where small groups of pupils engage in rich discussions about shared texts. Each participant contributes uniquely to the conversation by assuming different analytical roles, from summarising key points to exploring intriguing vocabulary. These focused discussions help pupils uncover deeper meanings within texts while developing critical thinking skills through collective exploration.

The think-pair-share method offers a structured way to engage all pupils in meaningful text analysis. Providing individual thinking time before moving into partner discussions ensures that even quieter pupils have opportunities to process their thoughts and contribute meaningfully to class discussions. When pairs later share their insights with the larger group, it creates a tapestry of diverse perspectives that enriches everyone's understanding of the text.

Jigsaw reading takes collaboration to another level by making each pupil responsible for teaching their peers a portion of the text. This approach ensures thorough comprehension of the material and helps pupils develop crucial communication skills as they learn to convey information to others effectively. Explaining concepts to classmates often deepens the original reader's understanding while helping others grasp new content.

The cooperative approach culminates in collaborative writing activities, where pupils work together throughout the writing process. Pupils learn to articulate their ideas clearly while considering different perspectives as they plan, draft and revise their work as a team. This shared writing experience helps pupils develop stronger organisational skills and produce more coherent written work, as they benefit from immediate peer feedback and diverse viewpoints throughout the creation process.

Equity and inclusion in cooperative literacy learning

Cooperative learning supports equity in literacy instruction by providing opportunities for all pupils to participate in reading and discussion, regardless of their skill level. When structured with clear expectations and roles, these strategies ensure that every pupil contributes to and benefits from the learning process.

Moreover, cooperative learning encourages peer modelling, where more proficient readers support developing readers in a way that fosters confidence and skill growth. This is particularly important in multilingual classrooms, where pupils may benefit from working alongside peers who share their home language or can model fluent reading in English.

Assessment and feedback in a cooperative learning environment

Assessment should be embedded within collaborative activities to maximise the benefits of cooperative learning. Teachers can use informal observations, group discussions and peer feedback to gauge pupil understanding. Additionally, formative assessments such as exit tickets, written reflections and pupil-led presentations provide insight into individual and group progress.

Moving forward: The power of collaboration in literacy education

Cooperative learning is a research-based approach that aligns seamlessly with the Science of Reading, providing pupils with engaging, interactive and supportive literacy experiences. By integrating cooperative strategies into reading instruction, educators create a dynamic learning environment where pupils actively construct knowledge, develop essential literacy skills and cultivate a lifelong love of reading. As schools prioritise evidence-based literacy practices, cooperative learning is a powerful tool for fostering engagement, equity and academic success.

> "Cooperative learning is a research-based approach that aligns seamlessly with the Science of Reading."

READING COLLABORATIONS
Peer-assisted learning
Literature circles
Think-pair-share for text analysis

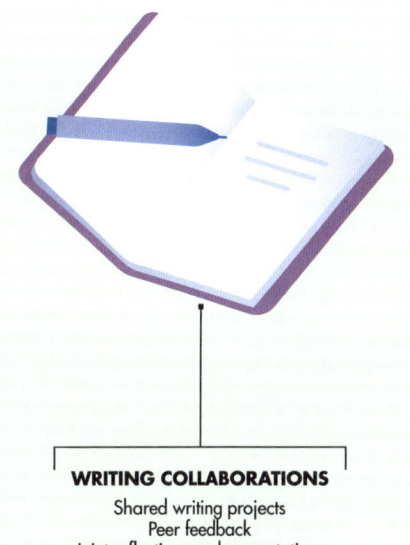

WRITING COLLABORATIONS
Shared writing projects
Peer feedback
Joint reflections and presentations

Small-Group Reading Instruction

by Elizabeth K. Waller

Learning to read is at the heart of education. Yet teaching children to read can be complex. Small-group reading instruction is a highly effective strategy for teaching reading skills.

Phonemic and phonological awareness are the basis for helping children learn to associate sounds with letters and words and eventually to decode words.

Word recognition is the beginning of reading instruction. However, reading is more than decoding and word recognition. Reading is a social activity, as defined by David Bloome (1985). This definition helped demonstrate the usefulness of a social structure known as small-group reading instruction, used to teach basic reading skills as well as higher-level reading and thinking skills. Reading connects pupils with the world around them. They need different approaches to learn the numerous skills that will make them successful readers, thinkers and learners.

Small-group instruction is one way that teachers can target individual pupil needs and deficits in reading skill development. When we consider reading as a social process, it makes sense that grouping for reading instruction can be very engaging and effective for learners.

Using assessment for setting up small groups

Strong assessments are necessary to determine pupils' abilities. Data from standardised testing, informal reading inventories and observations will help teachers identify pupils' weaknesses and strengths. These assessments and observations should also consider the cultural context, which will drive grouping for intervention, strategy instruction and more advanced reading skills beyond word recognition.

Forming small groups

Grouping should be flexible. This means that teachers should form groups using data from assessments and observations. Small groups allow and encourage pupils to interact with one another and the teacher.

Data drives how the teacher will reconfigure groups. Sometimes teachers will make groups heterogeneous and other times they will be homogeneous. With flexible grouping, struggling pupils will not feel stigmatised, because ability grouping is not the only criteria for grouping. Sometimes, they will be with pupils who have similar needs, while other times, they will be with pupils who have similar interests.

> "Small groups allow and encourage pupils to interact with each other and the teacher."

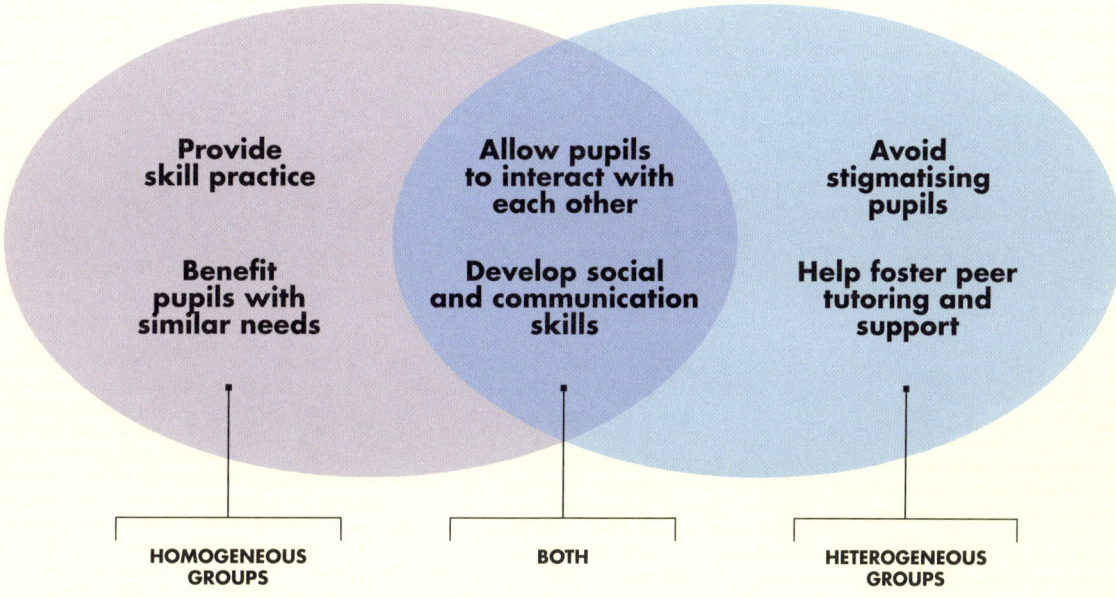

Homogeneous and heterogeneous small groups

- Provide skill practice
- Benefit pupils with similar needs

HOMOGENEOUS GROUPS

- Allow pupils to interact with each other
- Develop social and communication skills

BOTH

- Avoid stigmatising pupils
- Help foster peer tutoring and support

HETEROGENEOUS GROUPS

Small-group intervention

In small-group targeted intervention, teachers work with small groups of pupils who have similar reading instructional needs. For example, pupils may have deficits in decoding, fluency or comprehension.

Teachers can differentiate instruction to address specific areas where pupils need more support. This type of differentiation in small groups fosters comprehensive, customised, targeted support from teachers as well as active peer interaction and pupil engagement.

Strategy instruction

As pupils advance beyond language development, phonetic and phonemic awareness and decoding, small-group strategy instruction offers another social context where pupils can connect with their teachers and peers. Because strategy group work is targeted, the lessons are short and frequent.

Teachers can hone in on specific skills and may provide scaffolding such as asking guiding questions, modelling fluent reading, and using and encouraging think-alouds.

Small-group strategy sessions can help young pupils talk about what they are thinking. It will allow them to share perspectives and talk about the stories they read in a social setting that is engaging and inspiring.

In each of these scenarios, teachers must mastermind the delivery of instruction in these diverse small groups. Before the small-group planning begins, teachers must also plan for meaningful work for the rest of the class.

Using data to form and reconfigure the groups, planning and initiating the group activities, modelling successful reading behaviours and providing feedback on pupil performance rounds out effective small-group instructional planning.

The Gradual Release of Responsibility: Transforming Literacy Instruction

by Alexis Quinn Robinson

The Gradual Release of Responsibility model is a proven framework in literacy instruction. It transitions responsibility for learning from teacher to pupil, ensuring that pupils develop the skills, strategies and confidence to become independent readers.

The Gradual Release of Responsibility model (GRR) consists of four phases in a natural learning progression, where pupils start with observation and support before gradually becoming independent learners.

Phase 1: I do – Focused instruction

In this phase, the teacher explicitly models a literacy skill or strategy, often using think-alouds to demonstrate the cognitive processes involved in tasks like decoding, inferring or analysing text structure.

Phase 2: We do – Guided practice

After observing the teacher, pupils move into guided practice. Here, they work with the teacher to apply the skill or strategy. The teacher provides prompts, feedback and scaffolding to guide pupils as they practise.

Phase 3: You do together – Collaborative learning

During this phase, pupils practise the skill with peers in pairs or small groups. Collaborative activities, like literature circles, promote dialogue and problem-solving. This interaction helps pupils refine their understanding, as they discuss and negotiate ideas with others.

Phase 4: You do alone – Independent practice

In the final phase, pupils work independently to apply the skill or strategy. Tasks like reading comprehension questions, writing summaries or analysing text elements require pupils to demonstrate mastery. This stage is crucial for developing self-regulation and ensuring that pupils can apply their skills without support.

How GRR transforms literacy instruction

The GRR model promotes explicit skill development, ensuring that pupils receive clear, direct teaching of literacy skills. This is especially beneficial for struggling readers, English language learners and pupils with learning differences who may require more explicit guidance. It builds confidence and independence, helping pupils gain the skills and strategies to approach new texts and tasks with greater self-assurance.

GRR also allows teachers to customise instruction based on individual needs. During guided practice, for example, pupils who need extra support receive more scaffolding, while advanced learners can be challenged with more complex tasks. Another benefit is that GRR encourages pupils to reflect on their learning.

A model for the gradual release of responsibility

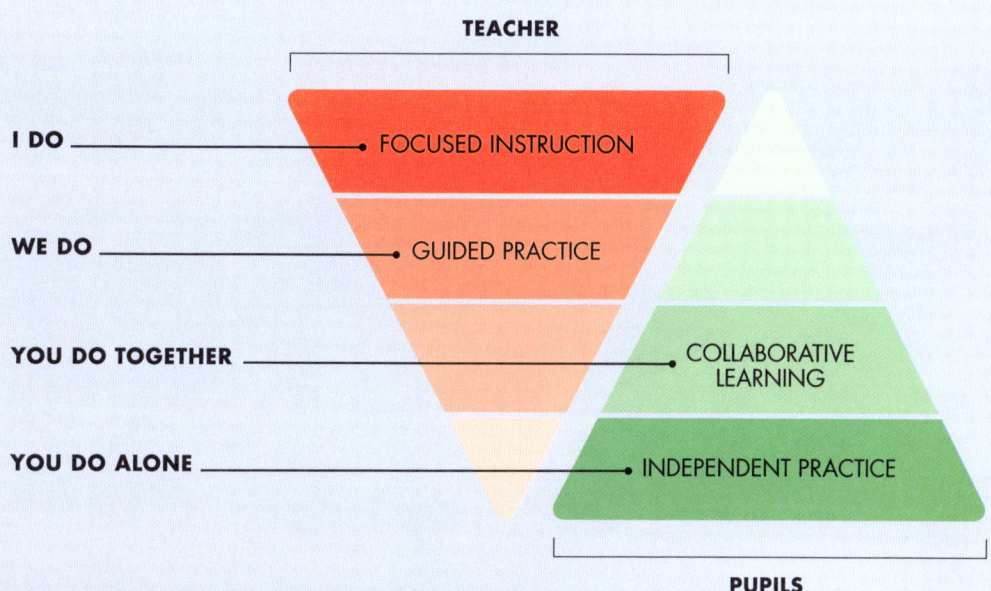

Teachers can model metacognitive strategies by asking questions such as, "What helped me understand this word?"

Conclusion

By gradually transitioning responsibility from teacher to pupil, GRR ensures that learners acquire the skills, strategies and independence necessary for lifelong reading success. GRR allows educators to meet the diverse needs of pupils while fostering confidence and competence. In an era where literacy is more important than ever, it equips pupils with the tools to thrive in a text-rich world, ensuring their success both in school and beyond.

Assessment and Feedback

THE GRR MODEL PROVIDES OPPORTUNITIES FOR FORMATIVE AND SUMMATIVE ASSESSMENT. Teachers observe pupils during guided practice and collaborative learning to gauge their understanding and offer immediate feedback. Independent tasks serve as summative assessments, showing whether pupils have mastered the targeted skills.

"Two very robust strategies to promote oral language are sharing conversations and interactive shared reading."

Jessica Bergeron

The Power of Explicit Instruction in Literacy

by Alexis Quinn Robinson

The Science of Reading has brought valuable insights for improving literacy outcomes, with explicit instruction standing out as a cornerstone of effective teaching.

Explicit instruction – characterised by systematic, direct and clear teaching – ensures pupils acquire essential reading skills. This article explores the core elements of explicit instruction, its role in literacy education and its impact on pupil development.

What is explicit instruction?

Explicit instruction is a structured approach to teaching that breaks complex skills into manageable steps. Unlike implicit methods that rely on pupils to infer concepts, explicit instruction provides direct, step-by-step guidance. Key characteristics include:

Explicit instruction offers a way to break down complex skills into steps.

Explicit instruction in literacy education

Clear learning objectives
Teachers clearly state the learning goals.

Direct modelling
Teachers demonstrate concepts, often using think-alouds.

Guided practice
Pupils practise skills with teacher supervision and immediate feedback.

Frequent checks for understanding
Continuous assessment ensures comprehension and adjusts instruction as needed.

Cumulative review
Skills are revisited to reinforce retention.

Building foundational skills
Reading is not natural; it must be taught. Explicit instruction is particularly effective for phonics and phonemic awareness — critical skills for decoding words. For instance, in phonics, teachers model letter-sound relationships and provide guided practice with words like *bat* or *bib*.

Supporting struggling readers
Explicit instruction benefits pupils with learning challenges, such as dyslexia, who struggle with pattern recognition. For example, breaking multisyllabic words into manageable parts helps these pupils decode complex texts.

Developing comprehension skills
Beyond decoding, explicit instruction is key to teaching comprehension strategies. Teachers model how to identify the main idea by thinking aloud, such as saying, "This sentence provides the key information about the topic."

Enhancing vocabulary and language development
Explicit instruction helps pupils learn vocabulary directly. Instead of inferring meanings, teachers teach word meanings and usage. For example, introducing the prefix *pre-* (meaning "before") and guiding pupils in using it with words like *preview* or *predict*.

How explicit instruction impacts learning

Explicit instruction promotes clarity and efficiency, ensuring that pupils understand the lesson's goals, minimising confusion and maximising learning time. Teachers can efficiently address literacy goals with clear, step-by-step guidance.

By providing clear expectations and frequent practice, explicit instruction also builds pupil confidence. Consistent feedback allows pupils to feel more successful and motivated.

How explicit instruction impacts teaching

Explicit instruction allows teachers to provide extra support to struggling pupils while challenging advanced learners. The cumulative nature of explicit instruction helps reinforce and enhance the retention of skills over time. Revisiting skills, such as decoding strategies, ensures pupils can apply their knowledge to new texts.

Explicit instruction aligns with evidence-based practices. The Science of Reading highlights the importance of explicit, systematic teaching. Studies show that this method is more effective than implicit teaching in improving literacy outcomes, particularly for early and struggling readers.

Best practices for implementing explicit instruction

To maximise the benefits of explicit instruction, educators can follow these best practices:

- Break skills into clear, sequential steps.
- Use think-alouds and visuals to clarify abstract concepts.
- Gradually reduce teacher assistance as pupils gain proficiency.
- Use questions and interactive activities to maintain engagement and ensure understanding.
- Use assessments to identify gaps and adjust instruction accordingly.

Conclusion

Explicit instruction is a powerful approach that drives literacy success by providing clarity, structure and systematic teaching. It ensures that all pupils, regardless of their starting point, acquire the skills needed to become proficient readers. This approach supports teachers in planning effective lessons and empowers pupils to overcome challenges, master foundational skills and become confident, independent readers. In an era where literacy is essential for personal and academic achievement, explicit instruction is crucial for unlocking every pupil's potential.

Defining Dyslexia

by Sarah Gannon and Alexandria Osburn

Dyslexia can impact pupils' vocabulary development, comprehension, and social-emotional functioning. What should educators and families understand about this learning disability?

Largely characterised by unexpected difficulties with accurate and/or fluent word recognition, dyslexia is the most common specific learning disability – a type of disability that can impact a person's ability to think, read, write, spell or do maths. The most widely accepted definition, written by the National Institute of Children Health and Human Development and endorsed by the International Dyslexia Association, states that dyslexia is "neurobiological in origin" and is "characterised by difficulties with accurate and/or fluent word recognition and by poor spelling and decoding abilities". The definition notes that these difficulties typically result from an unexpected deficit in the phonological component of language, in relation to other cognitive abilities and access to high-quality instruction. Further consequences may involve difficulties with reading comprehension and limited reading exposure, hindering vocabulary and background knowledge development.

Dyslexia is highly hereditary (Pennington and Olson, 2005). The neurobiological nature of dyslexia implies that the disability is present at

Matching instruction to dyslexia subtypes

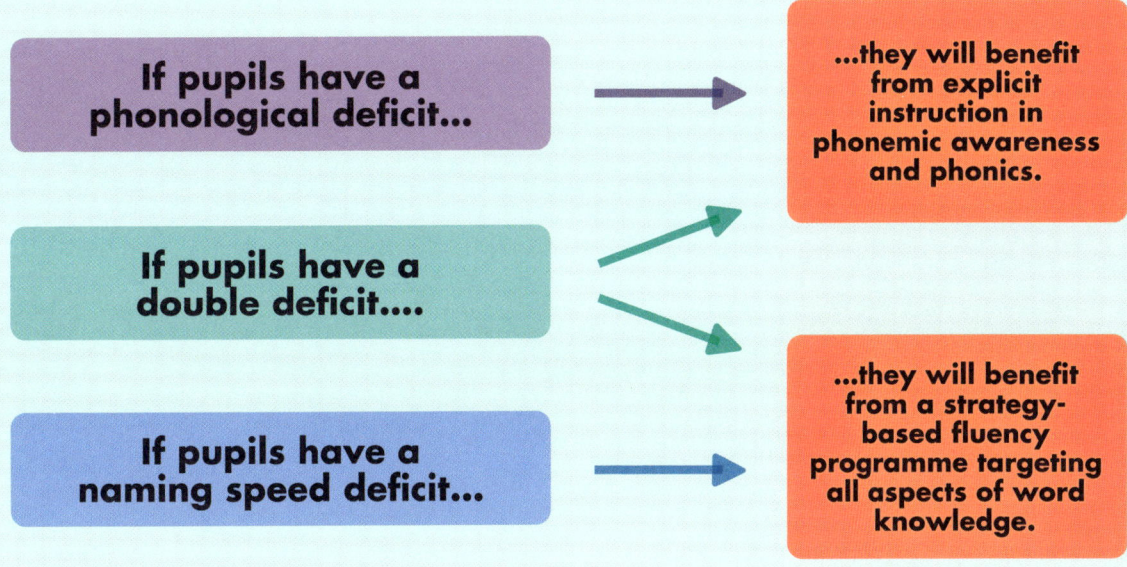

birth and related to the organisation and activation of brain cells responsible for processing sounds of language and visual symbols. Activation differences between typical readers and those with dyslexia are largely related to the brain cells in the area that efficiently connect letters and their corresponding sounds, called the visual word form area (Dehaene, 2011). As a result, dyslexia affects the ability to accurately pair letters with their corresponding sounds, resulting in impairments in decoding, sight word recognition, fluency and spelling.

Significance of subtypes

Both cognitive neuroscience and behavioural research have established that while dyslexia manifests differently in individuals, these variations can be categorised based on specific areas of difficulty. Over the past 20 years, research studies have identified distinct groups, or subtypes, of dyslexic pupils (Ozernov-Palchik et al., 2017; Wolf & Bowers, 1999). A phonological deficit and naming speed deficit are the two most common subtypes of dyslexia, and a combination of both results in what is known as a double-deficit subtype—often leading to more severe reading difficulties than those diagnosed with a single deficit. Pupils who present with a phonological deficit score below average on standardised measures of accuracy in phonemic awareness, decoding, sight word reading and passage reading. A naming speed deficit is characterised by below average performance on standardised measures of rapid automatised naming, particularly on subtests with letter naming, and measures of decoding, sight word and passage fluency.

Using a graphic organiser to arrange and analyse subtest scores from standardised assessments can help identify pupils with dyslexia and determine the subtype. Pupils with a phonological subtype benefit from explicit, systematic instruction to target accuracy in phonemic awareness and phonics while pupils with a naming speed deficit benefit from a strategy-based fluency programme targeting all aspects of word knowledge (Orkin et al., 2022). Research strongly suggests that for pupils to become fluent readers, they must develop automaticity not only in recognising letter-sound correspondences, but also in accessing word meanings, morphological knowledge and understanding how words function within sentences.

Pupils with double deficit dyslexia benefit from both explicit instruction in phonics as well as strategy-based fluency instruction using a multi-componential approach to target all aspects of word knowledge.

Impact on vocabulary and comprehension

The inability to accurately and/or fluently read a text often results in difficulties in comprehension due to reduced exposure to text and vocabulary. In a phenomenon coined the "Matthew Effect", pupils who experience early reading success are exposed to a greater number of texts which in turn enhances vocabulary growth, and builds background knowledge and comprehension. Conversely, children who struggle with reading early on are less likely to read, resulting in weaker vocabulary growth, diminished comprehension skills and a widening achievement gap over time. This creates a self-reinforcing cycle, where the "rich get richer" in literacy and the "poor get poorer". A shared understanding of dyslexia is critical in order to accurately identify pupils with the disability, effectively implement educational practices, and develop policies that support the educational community.

Dyslexia and screening

Children who experience initial challenges with reading rarely catch up to their peers in later year groups (Torgeson et al., 2001). One essential process in preventing reading failure is to screen pupils for risk of dyslexia and other reading difficulties. The majority of

> "The neurobiological nature of dyslexia implies that the disability is present at birth."

US states and countries such as the UK, the Netherlands and Finland have passed screening laws requiring school districts to screen pupils as early as Reception. Screening data offers helpful insights for schools to determine who is at risk, how significant is the risk and in what skill areas do pupils need support. Early identification can lead to targeted intervention, providing critical support for pupils in their educational journey.

Diagnosing dyslexia

Pupils experiencing persistent reading challenges should be referred for a comprehensive educational assessment in order to determine areas of strengths and weaknesses and to develop an Individualised Educational Plan (IEP). In addition to assessments that measure cognitive processes, districts should utilise a variety of tools to measure skills in the three domains of reading: accuracy, retrieval, or the ability to access and utilise information and oral language skills at the foundational level, single-word level and connected text level.

DYSLEXIA AFFECTS **5-17%** OF CHILDREN.

HERITABILITY RATES HOVER AROUND **50%** WHEN A FIRST-DEGREE RELATIVE, SUCH AS A SIBLING OR PARENT, REPORTS SUSPECTED OR DIAGNOSED DYSLEXIA.

Supporting Pupils with Dyslexia in the Classroom

by Lindsay Kemeny

Supporting pupils with dyslexia requires targeted instruction, accommodations and confidence-building. By fostering self-advocacy and maintaining high expectations, teachers can empower these learners.

Pupils with dyslexia are some of the most fragile learners in our classrooms and deserve the utmost respect, care and attention. Because the ability to read is so tightly connected to self-esteem, we need to be extra cautious in our words, attitudes and actions as we work with these pupils. Extra gentleness and patience are required. Here are some of my top recommendations to best support pupils with dyslexia in the classroom:

Provide effective reading instruction and intervention

Perhaps one of the most critical steps to take is to provide explicit and systematic reading and writing instruction. Unfortunately, many popular reading approaches are not effective for pupils who struggle with reading. Instead, these pupils need structured literacy teaching of basic language skills in order to become proficient readers. It's best if pupils receive this type of instruction in their general education classroom as well as in an intervention setting. Too often pupils receive instruction in a tutoring or intervention setting that is much different from or even contradicts what they are learning in their classroom. Consistency across settings will help pupils achieve the best results. Additionally, we need to ensure that pupils have plenty of opportunities to practise the skills they're being taught.

Provide accommodations

It can be easy to confuse interventions and accommodations, but it's important to realise that they are separate entities and that both are needed. Accommodations are how we support pupils by accounting for their challenges. I think of them as ways to remove the barriers that the learning disability causes. For example, allowing a pupil to listen to an audio version of an article removes the barrier of the child being unable to read the passage independently. This accommodation allows them to access the same information as the other pupils, but in a different way. It does not, however, directly address the deficit of being unable to read the passage on their own. The child still needs instruction to help remediate this barrier, and that is what the intervention does. It helps close the gap by addressing the specific need. We need to provide accommodations for our pupils with dyslexia, but we can't forget that they need intervention as well.

Some common accommodations for pupils include

- **using speech-to-text and text-to-speech software**
- **extra time on assignments and tests**
- **using audiobooks**
- **providing class notes**
- **not requiring pupils to read aloud in front of the whole class.**

INSTRUCTIONAL STRATEGIES AND EQUITY IN LITERACY 173

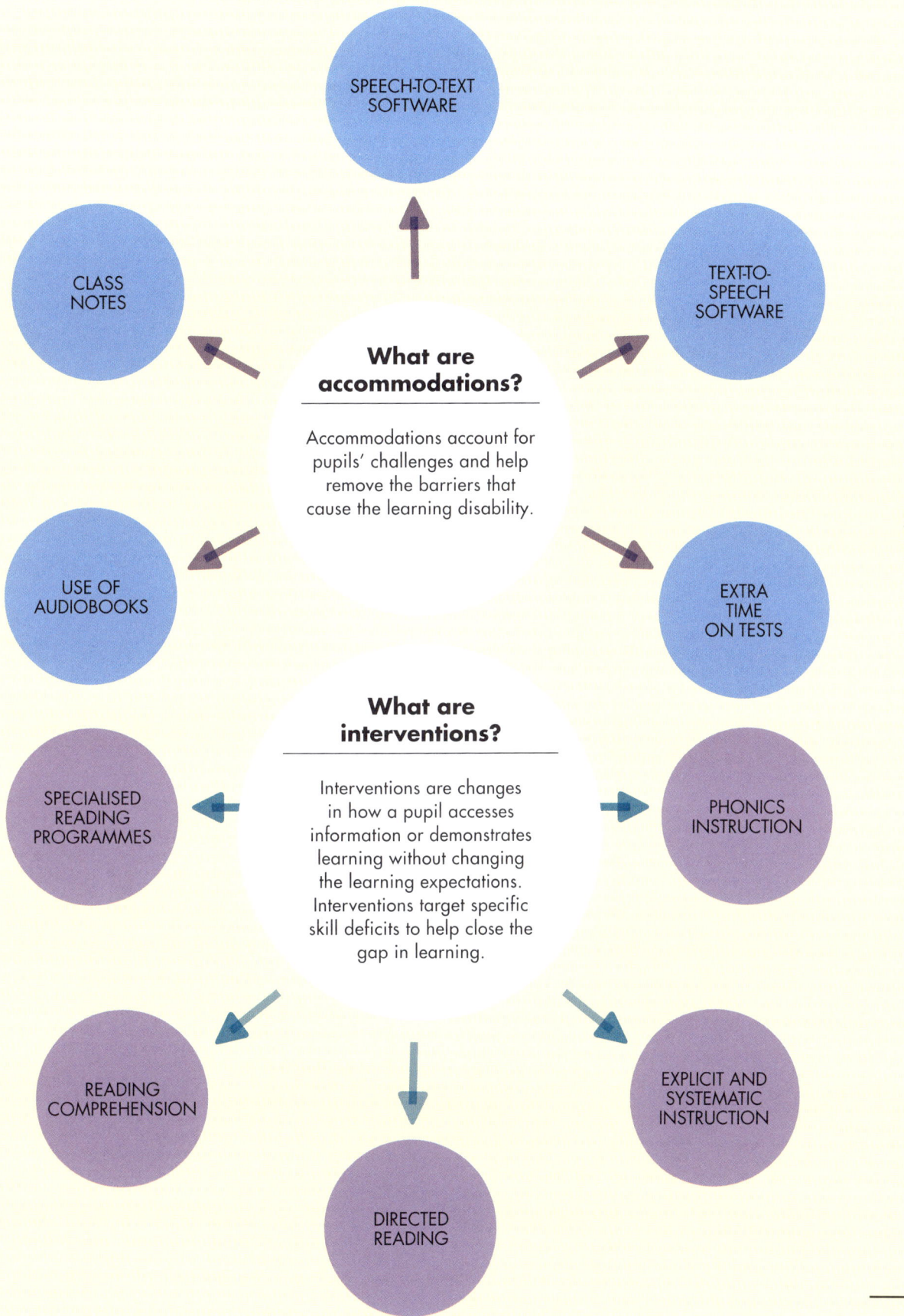

Teach them to advocate for themselves

It takes a lot of courage to stand up for yourself and let others know what you need. This can be especially difficult for a child who lacks confidence or has had negative experiences with this in the past. I remember encouraging my young son (with dyslexia) to talk to his teacher about the struggles and frustrations he was experiencing in the classroom. Before going to the teacher myself, I wanted him to understand what his Individualised Education Program (IEP) accommodations were and how to politely assert himself. I distinctly remember his small, pleading voice as he said, "But you're the one with the brave voice, Mom." He wasn't quite ready yet, and I knew he needed more help learning how to advocate for himself. So, I started bringing him with me to IEP meetings and teacher conferences. We talked about being polite but also assertive. We discussed his accommodations and why he needed them. We role-played different scenarios, where I would pretend to be his teacher, and he would practise speaking up for himself. Slowly, he started to advocate for himself. He is now in high school, and I remind him frequently that his teachers are still learning too. Sometimes he gets frustrated and exclaims, "Why am I the one who always has to teach them about dyslexia?" It can be quite a burden for a young pupil. Other times he's amazed at what the teachers already know. It's an ongoing process, but it's been rewarding to see him develop his own brave voice.

Providing tailored accommodations like audiobooks helps create an inclusive classroom environment, which can empower pupils with dyslexia to engage confidently in their learning.

> "It takes a lot of courage to stand up for yourself and let others know what you need."

Build confidence

The school environment can be overwhelming for some of our pupils with dyslexia. It's difficult to be in a place where you feel like you're failing. Many of these pupils have had negative and hurtful experiences related to their struggles learning to read. They feel inadequate and hopeless. They associate school with these negative emotions, here are some ways to change that:

- **Find ways to be positive with these pupils and help create more pleasant school experiences for them.**
- **Discover the things they do well and point them out to them every day.**
- **Help boost their confidence by frequently giving them genuine compliments about the things they do.**

I will never forget when my son's engineering teacher came to me and said, "THIS is his talent." He went on to explain my son's gift for engineering, giving me specific examples. Then he proceeded to explain future courses that I needed to make sure my son registered for so he could further develop his talent in this area. I will always appreciate that this teacher took the time to seek me out to let me know these things. Seeing the elated look on my son's face was priceless.

Keep expectations high

There's no reason why pupils with dyslexia can't soar as high as, and even higher than, other pupils in your class. Beware the crippling effect of low expectations. These pupils will rise to great heights if they are given the opportunity to. In a podcast interview, a young man with dyslexia wisely counselled, "Give us the opportunity to be great and we won't disappoint you" (Lambert, 2021). May we always remember to give these pupils the opportunity to be great.

Drawn to the Code: Hyperlexia and Reading

by Lori Fromowitz

Hyperlexia occurs when an individual has advanced early decoding skills that are usually significantly higher than their receptive language and reading comprehension skills.

Hyperlexia comes from the Greek words *hyper* ("over" or "above") and *lexia* ("word"). Though hyperlexia can be a standalone diagnosis, it frequently co-occurs in children who are autistic. Hyperlexia has been found across speakers of different languages, and children who are hyperlexic may demonstrate a preoccupation with letters and a love of text (Ostrolenk et al., 2017). These children may show a special interest in reckoning patterns in text. Of course, decoding is only one part of reading. A child who is sounding out words without comprehending them has not fully mastered reading. Both a skill and a disability, hyperlexia can be deceptive. Children who are hyperlexic often appear to read quite well because of their precocious ability to decode (or sound out) text, often well before the age of five. However, they may not comprehend the meaning behind the text they are decoding, especially as text becomes more challenging and the language comprehension demands increase.

Signs of hyperlexia

Hyperlexic children may decode text with high or advanced accuracy, even teaching themselves to decode without explicit instruction, at an early age. These children may show average or above average phonemic (speech sound) and phonological skills (Ostrolenk et al., 2017). Some of these children have an existing diagnosis of autism or demonstrate some characteristics similar to autism.

Another common characteristic of hyperlexic children is initial speech and language delays that improve at the onset of learning to decode. In some cases, children reportedly began talking after they started to decode words (Ostrolenk et al., 2017). These children may engage in echolalia, or speech repetition, or being Gestalt language processors, who process language

Potential areas to target when treating hyperlexic children

- Language, including grammar, vocabulary and word parts
- Applying background knowledge
- Recognising story parts such as characters and plot
- Understanding nonliteral language
- Inferencing

- Pragmatic language (language use, especially social application)
- Visualising text
- Understanding story and text structure
- Identifying author and character perspective
- Writing out "gestalts" or scripts

in chunks, rather than word by word (Meaningful Speech, 2023). They may also love or appear almost preoccupied with letters and reading – drawn to the code.

Hyperlexic children may have difficulties with the following:

- **comprehending oral and written language**
- **abstract thinking (Treffert, 2011)**
- **receptive or pragmatic language, particularly in the areas of inferencing, nonliteral language and perspective taking**
- **learning to decode more complex words (Ostrolenk et al., 2017)**

Treatment and strategies

Individuals who are hyperlexic will likely benefit from working with a speech language pathologist on both spoken and written language. If a child has difficulty with understanding receptive spoken language, they will often have difficulty understanding written language. A speech pathologist can work on all aspects of speech and language in order to help a child communicate orally and in written language, and a speech pathologist who is trained in literacy will be able to find the relationships between speech sounds, decoding, fluency and comprehension.

Strengths and motivations

A speech pathologist can recognise a child's strength in decoding and use this strength to build higher level skills, as well as engage in activities that are of high interest and motivating to the child. A holistic approach that addresses an understanding of their developmental continuum with respect to hyperlexia (Ostrolenk et al., 2017), as well as the individual's unique needs, strengths and interests, will support their reading comprehension over time.

ABOUT **84%** OF CHILDREN WHO HAVE HYPERLEXIA ARE ON THE AUTISM SPECTRUM.

ONLY **6-14%** OF CHILDREN WHO HAVE AUTISM ALSO HAVE HYPERLEXIA.

Specific Reading Comprehension Deficit

by Lori Fromowitz

A learner with this disability can decode (or sound out) written words but cannot understand the meaning of the text. Intervention strategies can assist learners with reading comprehension.

Successful reading requires the ability both to decode (sound out written words) and to interpret meaning from the text. Although reduced word decoding ability will also result in reduced reading comprehension, specific reading comprehension deficit (SRCD) occurs when a reader has at least average decoding skills but difficulty with interpreting meaning from the text or reading comprehension. Like other learning disabilities, SRCD is a neurodevelopmental condition, but is not caused by intellectual disability, vision or hearing problems, or neurological or physical injury.

Because the focus of early reading instruction begins with phonics and decoding, a specific reading comprehension deficit may not be apparent immediately. Pupils with SRCD may appear to be reading successfully during initial reading instruction when the focus is on decoding and then have difficulty later when the focus of reading instruction switches from gaining basic reading skills to the "reading to learn" stage, typically in Year 4 or 5 (Reading Rockets; Vanderbilt University). These pupils may fill in or guess words as they read out loud, skip lines when reading or read too rapidly (Tracht, 2022).

Oral language, executive function and reading comprehension

A reader with SRCD may demonstrate weaknesses or deficits in one or more areas of oral language, or demonstrate weaknesses in pragmatic or social language (Landi & Ryherd, 2017; Moats & Tolman, 2009). Some readers with SRCD may also have deficits in working memory and in attention and executive function (planning and organising), particularly in the area of cognitive flexibility, which is the ability to switch back and forth between aspects of a task. Reading requires balancing multiple abilities, including self-regulation, phonological awareness and linguistic skills. Readers must manage both decoding and meaning interpretation simultaneously (Cartwright et al., 2017).

Research and the Brain

NEUROIMAGING OF YOUNG READERS DEMONSTRATED A DIFFERENCE IN BRAINS AMONG YOUNG LEARNERS WHO HAVE READING DISABILITIES.

Brain imaging of individuals with word attack deficits are distinct from those of learners who have diagnoses of specific reading comprehension deficits (Vanderbilt University).

Frontal lobe
Associated with speech or phonemes

Parietal-temporal lobe
Associated with connecting phonemes and graphemes/letters

Temporal lobe
Associated with language comprehension

Temporal-occipital lobe
Associated with word recognition

Implications

Pupils with reading comprehension difficulties will likely have difficulty with answering comprehension questions, summarising text and inferencing. They will likely have difficulty with writing as reading demands become more difficult, particularly in response to written text. If a specific reading comprehends deficit is unidentified and untreated, reading comprehension can continue to be an area of difficulty in adulthood.

Intervention

If a pupil appears to struggle with reading comprehension, an evaluation that includes speech and language can help determine the area of deficit. Possible intervention strategies include the following:

- preview and review vocabulary
- make predictions and inferences
- review types and structures of text, key words, headings and captions
- practise summaries and retellings
- use graphic organisers or images to help readers interpret and visualise text (Landi & Ryherd, 2017)

Other strategies include teaching metacognition and relevant executive function strategies. Target areas of oral language such as morphology, grammar and syntax. Target reading fluency, including rate and expression. Some pupils may have mixed decoding and reading comprehension deficits. These pupils may benefit from intervention in both decoding and oral/written comprehension (Reading Rockets).

"When we equip every child with the ability to read, we build stronger, more informed communities."

Kareem Weaver

The alphabetic code

Consonant sound spellings

/j/
j	**j**et
g	**g**entle
ge	bar**ge**
dge	ju**dge**

/n/
n	**n**o
nn	pla**nn**ing
kn	**kn**ow
gn	**gn**at
pn	**pn**eumonia

/z/
z	**z**ip
zz	bu**zz**
s	i**s**
se	choo**se**
ze	snoo**ze**
x	**x**ylophone

/r/
r	**r**at
wr	**wr**ite
rr	ca**rr**y
rh	**rh**ino

/h/
h	**h**ot
wh	**wh**ole

/qu/ (/k/ + /w/)
qu	**qu**een

/t/
t	**t**in
tt	ge**tt**ing
ed	jump**ed**
bt	de**bt**
pt	**pt**erodactyl
te	defini**te**

/x/ (/k/ + /s/)
x	e**x**am

/y/
y	**y**es

/ng/
ng	si**ng**
n	pi**n**k

/s/
s	**s**ip
ss	gra**ss**
se	hou**se**
c	**c**ent
ce	voi**ce**
st	ca**st**le
sc	**sc**ience
ps	**ps**ychic

/v/
v	**v**ery
ve	ha**ve**

/ch/
ch	**ch**ip
tch	ma**tch**

/b/
b	**b**ig
bb	ra**bb**it

/th/ (voiced)
th	**th**at

/th/ (unvoiced)
th	**th**in

/f/
f	**f**an
ff	sta**ff**
ph	**ph**one
gh	lau**gh**
ffe	gira**ffe**

/w/
w	**w**ig
wh	**wh**en

/g/
g	**g**ot
gg	ju**gg**le
gh	**gh**ost

/d/
d	**d**og
ed	grabb**ed**
dd	mu**dd**le

/l/
l	**l**ip
ll	fu**ll**
le	app**le**
el	trav**el**
il	pup**il**
al	fin**al**
ol	id**ol**

/sh/
sh	**sh**op
ch	ma**ch**ine
s	**s**ugar
ti	ini**ti**al
ci	spe**ci**al

/p/
p	**p**ot
pp	ha**pp**y

/m/
m	**m**an
mm	su**mm**er
mb	la**mb**
mn	Autu**mn**

/k/
k	**k**ite
c	**c**at
ck	du**ck**
ch	**ch**ord
que	anti**que**
q	Ira**q**

/zh/
s	lei**s**ure
ge	presti**ge**
z	sei**z**ure

The alphabetic code

Vowel sound spellings

/ear/
- ear   near
- eer   deer
- ere   here

/ae/
- a   table
- ai   rain
- a–e   game
- ea   great
- ay   say
- ey   they
- ei   vein
- aigh straight
- eigh eight

/er/
- er   her
- ur   turn
- ir   girl
- or   world
- ear   learn
- our   colour
- ar   collar
- re   centre
- yr   zephyr

/ow/
- ow   cow
- ou   out
- ough drought

/i/
- i   in
- y   myth

/oi/
- oi   join
- oy   boy

/o/
- o   not
- a   was

/or/
- or   for
- our   your
- a   ball
- al   walk
- ore   more
- oor   door
- aw   lawn
- au   fraud
- oar   board
- ar   warm
- ough fought
- augh daughter

/oo/
- oo   cook
- oul   could
- u   put

/ue/
- u–e   tune
- u   pupil
- ew   few
- ue   cue

/a/
- a   cat

/ie/
- i   wild
- ie   pie
- i–e   like
- igh   night
- y   dry
- eigh height

/oa/
- oa   boat
- ow   grow
- o   most
- o–e   note
- oe   toe
- ough though
- ou   soul
- ew   sew

/ear/
- ear   near
- eer   deer
- ere   here

/air/
- air   chair
- are   dare
- ear   bear
- eir   their
- ere   where
- ayor mayor
- ayer prayer
- ae   aerosol

/u/
- u   tub
- ou   touch
- o   Monday
- oo   blood

/ee/
- e   me
- ee   meet
- ea   seat
- e–e   eve
- ie   chief
- y   funny
- ey   key
- ei   receive
- i   variation
- eo   people

/e/
- e   bed
- ea   bread
- ai   said
- ie   friend
- eo   leopard

/ar/
- ar   jar
- a   glass
- al   calm
- er   clerk
- ear   heart

/oo/
- oo   boot
- ue   blue
- ew   grew
- u   super
- ui   suit
- u–e   flute
- ou   soup
- oe   shoe
- o   do
- ough through

Debunking Reading Myths: A Clear Path to Literacy

by Dr. Chase Young

The foundation of learning in school generally seems to emanate from a child's learned ability to read. Several prevailing fallacies about effective reading instruction create a barrier to evidence-based practice that could hold pupils back from progress. Confronting these misconceptions means clarity of concept, founded in research and practical experience to afford all learners equal opportunity toward success in literacy.

MYTH 1
Reading is like speaking–it's natural

Reality check: Reading is not innate. While speaking will develop naturally by pupils being around others and imitating them, reading must be taught explicitly. It is a process of training the brain to connect written symbols to sounds; this process requires explicit instruction. This distinction highlights the importance of systematic instruction for developing proficient readers.

MYTH 2
If children are surrounded by books, they will learn to read

Reality check: While exposure to books is helpful in developing an appreciation for reading and in building background knowledge, it is not enough. Children need explicit phonics and phonemic awareness instruction to decode words proficiently and to become fluent readers. Immersion has to be complemented by focused teaching, so that pupils have the means to access written text independently.

MYTH 3
Skilled readers do not use decoding

Reality check: Even accomplished readers decode material, but such readers have developed it to the stage where it often appears to require no effort at all. Decoding is the fundamental basis of fluent reading, and word recognition automaticity is gained through much repetition. Proficiency is achieved gradually through consistent application, meaning that structured practice is indeed essential in order to develop it.

MYTH 4
Memorising sight words is superior to phonics instruction

Reality check: Sight words do play a role in reading fluency, but mastery of them is based on decoding rather than rote memorisation. Phonics instruction helps pupils recognise patterns and apply them to unfamiliar words, ensuring a deeper understanding.

MYTH 5
Some children are not "wired" to read

Reality check: All but a very few children can be taught to read if provided appropriate instruction and support. Some pupils may encounter difficulties due to dyslexia or other learning differences; however, targeted evidence-based interventions, combined with individual accommodations, make literacy attainable. This myth greatly diminishes pupil potential and fails to acknowledge the effectiveness of specialised instructional strategies.

MYTH 6
Comprehension strategies comprise the bulk of reading instruction

Reality check: Comprehension strategies are valuable, but they have to be grounded in decoding, fluency and vocabulary. Without these latter parts, the comprehension strategies alone don't take the pupil anyplace. In good reading instruction, all of the components are integrated to create a coherent approach that supports deep understanding of texts.

MYTH 7
Poor readers need more practice

Reality check: Practice alone does not solve the root problems struggling readers face. It is quality instruction, linked to diagnostic assessments that identify what pupils know and don't know, that provides the pathway to complete literacy. Evidence-based interventions provide ways to target these root causes and make actual progress.

MYTH 8
Fluency is best built by having pupils read aloud in class

Reality check: Cold readings in front of peers are not only counterproductive, but often cause a great amount of stress, limiting the chances of further development of reading skills. Rather, fluency is developed through multiple readings, guided practice and constructive feedback. Such practices give pupils the confidence and ability to read accurately and expressively. And remember, reading is not a race – the goal of fluent reading is not to read fast; it is to read at an appropriate pace with expression that matches the meaning of the text.

MYTH 9
Graphic novels and audiobooks are not "real" reading

Reality check: Graphic novels and audiobooks are valid paths to literacy. Graphic novels can help pupils build comprehension by integrating visual and textual elements, while audiobooks develop listening comprehension-one of the most foundational literacy skills. These can also engage different types of learners and widen access to literature.

MYTH 10
Phonics instruction stifles creativity and enjoyment

Reality check: Far from making pupils less creative, phonics instruction frees their creativity because it allows pupils to read with fluency and independence. The reader who decodes text easily is free to pay attention to deeper meaning in the reading and thus develop a true love for reading and to increase imagination. Phonics lessons can also be interactive and fun to encourage learning.

Final words: We can do it

By tackling these myths with evidence and intention, we can forge an informed and effective approach to literacy education. It is within our collective power as educators, administrators and policymakers to make sure that every pupil leaves school a confident and capable reader. Reading instruction doesn't have to be a mystery. It's not magic; it's evidence, effort, and engagement. We can rewrite this narrative together, one myth at a time.

Jargon Buster

These terms and concepts are key for implementing principles of the Science of Reading in your classroom or at home.

CLOSE READING
examining a text closely, often through reading it multiple times and examining it in detail

COLLECTIVE EFFICACY
the belief that a group of people, working together, can achieve a shared outcome

CULTURALLY RESPONSIVE EDUCATION
an approach to teaching that involves recognising and incorporating the variety of children's cultural experiences and backgrounds

DECODING
the ability to translate written symbols into sounds, allowing readers to recognise words

DIAGNOSTIC ASSESSMENTS
tests or evaluations used to identify pupils' strengths and weaknesses, often used to identify areas where pupils need support

ENCODING
the process of breaking a spoken word into its individual sounds in order to write or spell it

EQUITY IN EDUCATION
the idea that all children have a right to learn, and that addressing gaps in literacy requires overcoming barriers

FLUENCY
the ability to read text with automaticity

FORMATIVE ASSESSMENTS
low-stakes assessments used to measure pupils' learning and adjust instruction

GENRE STUDY
the study of types of writing and their typical forms or conventions

GRAPHEME
the smallest unit in a system of writing (such as a letter)

GROWTH MINDSET
the belief that people's abilities are not fixed but can change and grow

HIGH-FREQUENCY WORDS
the words that occur most frequently in text, also known as sight words

LANGUAGE COMPREHENSION
the ability to understand spoken language, including vocabulary, syntax and background knowledge

LITERATURE CIRCLE
a group of pupils who meet to discuss a book, with each pupil taking on a role in the group

MORPHOLOGY
the study of how words are formed

ORTHOGRAPHY
the set of spelling conventions of a language

PHONEME
the smallest unit of sound used in spoken English

PHONEME MANIPULATION
the ability to add, delete, and substitute sounds (or phonemes) to create new words

PHONEMIC AWARENESS
the ability to identify and manipulate phonemes or sounds

PHONICS
the process of matching spoken sounds to letters or groups of letters

PRAGMATICS
the ability to share and understand a message across contexts, incorporating all components of language including unstated aspects (such as nonliteral language, facial expressions and tone of voice)

READING LEVEL
a measure of a pupil's ability to read, often used to identify appropriate texts or educational approaches

SEGMENTING
the ability to divide or break up words into individual sounds

SEMANTIC MAPPING
a way of graphing or mapping relationships between words

SEMANTICS
the study of the meanings of words

SUMMATIVE ASSESSMENT
testing or evaluation that measures pupils' learning at the end of a year or unit

SYNCHRONOUS PAIRED ORAL READING TECHNIQUES
a set of methods for shared reading involving a child and a tutor, such as an adult or more proficient peer

TEXT STRUCTURE
the way an author organises information in a text

WORD LADDER
a word game involving chains of related words, with each word in a chain differing in one letter or sound from the words immediately before and after

AUTOMATICITY
the ability to recognise and decode words quickly and accurately

PEER-ASSISTED LEARNING
a type of collaborative learning in which pupils help peers master the subject matter

SYNTAX
the arrangement of words and phrases to create sentences in a language

PHONOLOGICAL AWARENESS
the ability to recognise and manipulate the sounds of spoken language

Index

A

accommodations 172–173
accuracy 56, 57, 58, 59, 84
Adams, M. J. 40
adding sounds to make a new word 48, 50, 51
AI 91
AIMSweb 120
alliteration 27–28
alphabet knowledge 40–41
alphabetic code 23, 32, 182–183
alphabetic phase 18–19
alphabetic principle 8
Amazing Grace (Hoffman, 1991) 95
angular gyrus 8–9
arcuate fasciculus 9
assessment
   blending phonemes 128
   cooperative learning 159
   cultural awareness 143
   diagnostic assessment 128, 133, 171
   Dynamic Indicators of Basic Early Literacy Skills (DIBELS) 120, 121, 128–129
   fluency 56, 57, 58–59, 120–121, 128
   formative assessment 124–126, 133
   frequency of 121
   high-frequency words (HFWs) 42
   high-stakes assessments 133
   phonemic awareness 25
   small-group reading instruction 160
   summative assessment 132–133
   think-alouds 140–141
attraction theory 78–81
audiobooks 185
authenticity 85, 91
autism 100, 177
automaticity
   brain structures 9
   decoding 12
   and fluency 57, 59
   letter recognition 40–41
   orthographic mapping 24

B

background knowledge 14, 67, 81, 91, 140, 142
baseline data 120, 133
behavioural factors in reading engagement 80–81
biliteracy 102–105
blending chunks 83
blending phonemes 8, 48–51, 128
Bloome, D. 160
book clubs 88–89
brain structures 8–9, 78, 99

C

cerebellum 9
challenge, appropriate levels of 77
challenging books 64
chapter books 64
choice of books 64, 77, 81, 143
chunking 52–53, 67, 68, 69, 83
Clay, M. M. 40
close reading 66–67 *see also* interrupted reading
co-constructed writing 39
cognitive dissonance 80
cognitive factors in reading engagement 78
Colenbrander, D. 43
collaboration *see also* group work
   book clubs 88–89
   collaborative vocabulary learning 62
   cooperative learning 154–156
   Gradual Release of Responsibility (GRR) model 162
   literature circles 89
   motivation for reading 77
   Response to Intervention (RTI) 123
   strengthening literacy 157–159
Common Underlying Proficiency 102, 104
communities of readers 81
comprehension
   assessment 128
   checking understanding 58, 167
   close reading 66–67
   cultural understanding 142
   dyslexia 170
   and expression 58
   and fluency 46, 56, 58
   hyperlexia 177
   instructional approaches 13
   multisyllabic words 82
   myths 185
   oral language development 106, 107
   pragmatics 100
   as purpose of reading 59
   reading engagement 78
   reading motivation 76

Reading Rope model 14
reading volume 91
repetition 85
Simple View of Reading (SVR) 12–13
speaking skills 98
specific reading comprehension deficit (SRCD) 178–179
vocabulary 60–62
consolidated alphabetic phase 19
context clues 60
cooperative learning 154–159
correct words per minute (CWPM) 120
critical thinking 67, 68, 113, 117
cultural differences 100, 142–143
culture, school 146
curiosity 80, 81
curriculum-based measures (CBMs) 120

D

data-driven decision-making 123, 129, 132–133, 138, 160
decodable readers (texts) 33–35
decoding
  and the brain 8
  hyperlexia 176
  interrupted reading 68
  long words 43, 73, 82–84
  myths 184
  oral language development 149
  orthographic mapping 24
  phonetic decoding 23
  phonics 32
  pragmatics 100

reading levels 18–19
Reading Rope model 15
Simple View of Reading (SVR) 12–13
word ladders 37
deconstruction/reconstruction of texts 68, 69
deletion of sounds to make a new word 48, 50, 51
diacritical marks 58
diagnostic assessment 128, 130, 133, 171
Discrepancy Model 145
discussion-based reading activities 157
Dolch, E. W. 42
"Don't Skip It" strategy 95
Downs, J. 70, 85, 91
Dynamic Indicators of Basic Early Literacy Skills (DIBELS) 120, 121, 130–131
dyslexia 169–175

E

early identification of reading difficulties 121, 123, 171
early reading stages 8–9
Elder, L. 68
Elkonin boxes 25, 38
emotional factors in reading engagement 81
encoding 38–39
engagement, reading 78–81
English Alphabetic Code 23, 32, 182–183
English Language Learners 141, 158, 162 see also biliteracy

English spelling 30
equity 144–148, 158
errors 19, 99, 121
etymology 60
executive function 101, 178
experiential knowledge 81
explicit instruction 13, 25, 59, 90, 115–116, 166–168
expression 56, 58, 114

F

family contribution to development of skilled readers 149–151
  see also parents
fiction narrative text structures 94–95
fine motor skills 9
fluency 56–59
  assessment 56, 57, 58–59, 120–121, 128
  biliteracy 102
  brain structures 9
  and comprehension 46, 56, 58
  consolidated alphabetic phase 19
  defining 56
  explicit instruction 59
  high-frequency words (HFWs) 42
  oral fluency 70
  phonics instruction 33
  phonological awareness 26
  pragmatics 100
  and reading aloud 185
  repetition 85
  word recognition 46

formative assessment 126–128, 133
frequency of letters 40
frontal lobe 8, 9, 99, 179
Fry, E. 42
fundamental right, literacy as 144–148

G

games 31, 37, 46, 112–114
genre study 92–93
genre wheels 71
genres, introducing a variety of 64, 71, 78, 92–93
Gestalt language processors 176–177
gists/ten-word takeaways 73
Glaser, D. A. 56, 59
goal-setting 120
Golem effect 145
Gradual Release of Responsibility (GRR) model 162–163
grammar and syntax
   modelling 108
   oral language development 106
   Reading Rope model 15
   syntactic play 112
graphemes 23
graphic novels 64, 185
graphic organisers 80, 95
group work
   book clubs 88–89
   cooperative learning 154–156, 157
   formative assessment 125
   small-group reading instruction 160–161
growth mindsets 146
guided practice 162, 167

H

Hasbrouck, J. 56, 57, 58, 59, 120
"heart words" 43
Hiebert, E. H. 82–83
high-frequency words (HFWs) 42–43, 46
highlighters 67
high-quality teaching 145
high-stakes assessments 133
history of writing systems 22, 38
home-school partnership 143, 149
human rights 144–145
hyperlexia 176–177

I

I do-We do-You do-You do alone 162
illustrated books 64
independent reading 63–65
Individualised Educational Plans (IEPs) 171, 174
inferences 15
informal learning 41
input scaffolding 137
intensive interventions 122, 127
interactive read-alouds 108
interactive writing 39
interests, finding books that cater to children's 64, 71, 77
interrupted reading 68–69
interventions
   dyslexia 172, 173
   Multi-Tiered Systems of Support 127
   progress monitoring 121
   Response to Intervention (RTI) 122–123
   small-group reading instruction 160
   specific reading comprehension deficit (SRCD) 179
intonation 53, 100 *see also* prosody
intrinsic motivations for reading 76
irregular words 30, 42, 43

J

jigsaw activities 156, 158
jokes and riddles 112–114

K

Katzir-Cohen, T. 59
Kilpatrick, D. A. 25

L

language disorders 100 *see also* reading disabilities
language play 112–114
language-rich environments 108, 150
leadership 146
left side of the brain 9
lesson planning 138, 146, 161
letter boxes 38
Letter Naming Fluency (LNF) 129
letter recognition 40–41
letter sorting tasks 41
leveled books 35
Liberman, I. Y. 27
linguistic interdependence 102
linguistic resources, utilising all 104
Lippitt–Knoster Model of Change 146, 147

listening skills 106
literacy environments 78
literacy knowledge 15, 73
literary devices 66
literature circles 89
Loftus, M. 60
logos and signs, recognition of 18
long words 43, 73, 82–84
long-term memory 9, 18, 24
love for reading, fostering 63–65
low expectations, combatting 145
low literacy levels 145, 148

M

magnetic letters 41, 50
"Matthew Effect" 170
MAZE test 128
McClelland, J. L. 40
meaning
   ascription of 35
   brain structures 8–9
   and connections 60
   explicit instruction 115
   focus on 31
   Reading Rope model 15
   semantics 115–117
   vocabulary 60–62
mental dictionary 30
metacognition 80, 140, 179
"mispronunciation correction" 43
mixed ability group work 154–156
modelling 39, 67, 84, 108, 140–141, 167
morphology
   high-frequency words (HFWs) 43
   language play 112

multisyllabic words 82, 83
oral language development 106
strategies to figure out new words 60
Morrison, J. D. 68–69
motivation for reading 76–77, 78–81
multimodality 81, 93
multisyllabic words 73, 82–84
Multi-Tiered Systems of Support 122–123, 127

N

names, learning to recognise own 40
naming speed deficits 169
National Assessment of Educational Progress (NAEP) levels 57, 82
neural pathways 8–9, 52
nonfiction 64, 92, 94, 95
nonliteral language 101
non-narrative structures 94
Nonsense Word Fluency-Correct Letter Sounds (NWF-CLS) 128
Nonsense Word Fluency-Words Recorded Correctly (NWF-WRC) 128
non-traditional reading formats 64, 81, 185
norm-referenced assessment 133
nuanced meanings 115

O

occipital lobe 9, 99, 179
onset-rime structure 28, 52–53
oral language development 106–109, 149

Oral Reading Fluency-Words Correct (ORF-WC) 128
ORF norms 57
orthographic knowledge 29–31
orthographic mapping 24, 25, 32
Ortlieb, E. 78
output scaffolding 137

P

Paige, D. D. 25
paired oral reading 70–73
parents
   cultural understanding 143
   family contribution to development of skilled readers 149–151
   orthographic knowledge 31
   Reading Rope model 17
   supporting close reading 67
parietal lobe 9, 99, 179
partial alphabetic phase 18
Paul, R. 68
peer feedback 125, 157, 159
peer tutoring 70–73, 156
peer-assisted learning 157
performing texts 85, 91
personal narrative texts 93
phonemes
   blending phonemes 8, 48–51
   decoding 22, 23, 28
   encoding 25
   phoneme manipulation skills 25, 48–51, 107
   phoneme substitution activities 51
   phonemic awareness 8, 22–25, 26, 49, 103

phonemic inventory of English 23
segmentation 23, 48
phonetic decoding 23
phonics instruction 29, 32–35
   assessment 128
   decoding 13
   myths 184, 185
   reading levels 18–19
   speaking skills 99
phonological awareness 26–28
   language play 112
   learning a second language 103, 104
   oral language development 107
   reading aloud to children 17
   Reading Rope model 15
phonological deficits 169
phonological play 112
phonological processing 9
phonological umbrella 27
picture-sorting activities 28
planning 138, 146, 161
play-based learning 109
pleasure, reading for 63–65
poetry 93
practice 41, 43, 84, 185
pragmatics 100–101
pre-alphabetic phase 18
Precision Teaching 120
predictions 30, 140
prefixes 83, 84
professional development 123
progress monitoring 120–121, 129
pronunciation practice 62, 98
prosody 58, 100 see also expression
punctuation 58

R

Rasinski, T. V. 58
rate of reading 56, 57
"Read Like Us" 85, 91
read-alouds 35, 108
reader's theatre 85, 91
reading aloud by children 19, 58–59, 185
reading aloud to children 17, 19, 67, 73, 98, 108, 114, 150
reading aloud with children 70–73
reading difficulties 121–123, 128, 162, 176–177, 178–179
reading disabilities 133, 169–175
reading goals, personal 81
reading levels 18–19
Reading Rope model 13, 14–17, 89, 115
reading spaces, comfortable 65
reading volume 90–91, 184
readworks.org 91
recommending books to children 64
repetition 62, 72, 85, 91, 121
Response to Intervention (RTI) 122–123
revision of new words 62
rhymes 109, 114, 143
rhyming 27, 52–53
rich conversations 35, 150
rich language environments 108, 150
rich texts 60, 68
rime blending 27, 28
Rumelhart, D. E. 40

S

Sappington, L. 60
scaffolding 51, 71, 84, 90, 136, 161
Scarborough, H. 13, 14–17, 115
Scheifele, U. 76
schwa 83
scope and sequence of instruction 33
screening for reading difficulties 123, 129, 171
second language learning 102–105
   see also English Language Learners
segmentation 23, 25, 27, 48
self-assessment 126
self-determination theory 76
self-teaching hypothesis 24
semantic mapping 60, 61, 116–117
semantic play 112
semantics 9, 115–117
sentence frames 139
serve-and-return dialogue 73
"shared pen" technique 39
sharing texts 70–73, 150
short-term memory 9
sight recognition 15, 184
Simple View of Reading (SVR) 12–13, 14, 115
small-group reading instruction 160–161
social activity, reading as 77, 78–79, 113–114, 160
songs 52, 109, 114, 143
sound boxes 25, 38
"sounding it out" strategy 46, 48–51, 52
speaking skills 98–99 see also oral language development

special education pupils 141, 162
    see also reading disabilities
specific reading comprehension deficit (SRCD) 178–179
speech language pathology 101, 177
"speed" of reading 56, 57
spelling 29–31, 33, 84, 182–183
storytelling 109, 114
Stouffer, J. 38
"Strive-for-Five" 17, 73
suffixes 43, 83, 84
summarising text skills 73
summative assessment 132–133
superior temporal gyrus 8
syllables
    clapping syllables 28
    phonological awareness 26
    rime blending 27
    syllabication strategies 43
    syllable blending 27
Synchronous Paired Oral Reading Techniques (SPORT) 70–73
syntax see grammar and syntax
systematic instruction 33

T

targeted interventions 122–123, 127
"Teatime Reading Fridays" 65
temporal lobe 9, 99, 179
ten-word takeaways 73
text structures 19, 94–95
text to speech 22–23, 172
textproject.org 91
text-rich environments 46

think-alouds 80, 139, 140–141
think-pair-share 89, 155, 157–158
three-read method 66–67
Tindal, G. 56, 57, 58, 120
tongue twisters 112, 114
translanguaging 104
trends measurement 120
Triple A fluency instruction 59
Turner, J. 77

U

Uh-oh…Phew! graphic organiser 95

V

verbal reasoning 15
visual memory 29
visual representations of close reading journey 67
visual word form area (VWFA) 9
visualisation of a text 140
vocabulary
    and comprehension 13
    direct instruction 60
    dyslexia 170
    explicit instruction 116
    high-frequency words (HFWs) 42–43, 46–47
    language play 112
    learning a second language 104
    oral language development 106
    Reading Rope model 14
    reading volume 90
    strategies to figure out new words 60

teaching 60–62
    vocabulary continua 60–61
    word ladders 37
volume of reading, increasing 90–91
Vygotsky, L. 77

W

What if You Had Animal Eyes (Markle, 2017) 95
White, S. 57
whiteboards 41, 50
whole-word recognition 99
Why We Can't Wait (King, 1964) 68
Wolf, M. 59
word chains/word ladders 36–37, 49
word families 49, 50
word games 31, 37, 46, 112–114
word hunts 31
word ladders/word chains 36–37, 50
word recognition 12, 14, 46–47
word sorting tasks 31
word studies 49, 50
word walls 46
word-learning strategies 60
words correct per minute (WCPM) 57
Write It Out strategy 38
writing skills 38–39, 107
writing systems 22, 38

Z

Zone of Proximal Development 77
Zutell, J. 58

Bibliography

Adams, M. J. (1990). *Beginning to read: Thinking and learning about print*. MIT Press.

Ambarchi, Z., Boulton, K. A., Thapa, R., Arciuli, J., DeMayo, M. M., Hickie, I. B., Thomas, E. E., & Guastella, A. J. (2024). Social and joint attention during shared book reading in young autistic children: A potential marker for social development. *Journal of Child Psychology and Psychiatry, 65*(11), 1441-1452.

Aukerman, M., & Chambers Schuldt, L. (2021). What matters most? Toward a robust and socially just science of reading. *Reading Research Quarterly*, 56(1), 85-103.

Blain-Brière, B., Bouchard, C., & Bigras, N. (2014). The role of executive functions in the pragmatic skills of children age 4–5. *Frontiers in Psychology*, 5, 240.

Bloome, D. (1985). Reading as a social process. *Language Arts, 62*(2), 134–142.

Brenner, D., & Hiebert, E. H. (2010). If I follow the teachers' editions, isn't that enough? Analyzing reading volume in six core reading programs. *The Elementary School Journal, 110*(3), 347–363.

Broughton, A. J., Przymus, S. D., Ortiz, A. A., & Cruz, B. J. S. (2023). Critical consciousness in decision-making: A model for educational planning and instruction with bilingual/multilingual students with disabilities. *TEACHING Exceptional Children*, 55(5), 338-349.

Brown, S. & Kappes, L. (2012). Implement the Common Core State Standards: A primer on "close reading of text". *Aspen Institute Education and Society Program*.

Brown, L. T., Mohr, K. A. J., Wilcox, B. R., & Barrett, T. S. (2018). The effects of dyad reading and text difficulty on third-graders' reading achievement. *The Journal of Educational Research*, 111(5), 541–553.

Burch, J. (2023, November 9). *Affirming neurodivergence: No more 'quiet hands'*. The ASHA LeaderLive.

Cabell, S. Q., & Zucker, T. A. (2024). Using strive-for-five conversations to strengthen language comprehension in preschool through grade one. *The Reading Teacher*, 77(4), 522–532.

Calderón, M., August, D., Durán, D., Madden, N., R. Slavin & M. Gil (2003). *Spanish to English transitional reading: Teacher's manual*. Baltimore, MD: The Success for All Foundation.

Cartwright, K.B., Coppage, E.A., Lane A.B., Singleton, T., Marshall T.R., and Bentivegna, C. (2017). Cognitive flexibility deficits in children with specific reading comprehension difficulties. *Contemporary Educational Psychology,* 50, 33-44.

Catts, H. W., Hogan, T. P., & Fey, M. E. (2003). Subgrouping poor readers on the basis of individual differences in reading-related abilities. *Journal of Learning Disabilities*, 36(2), 151–164.

Clay, M. M. (1991). *Becoming literate: The construction of inner control*. Heinemann.

Clay, M. M. (2005). *Literacy lessons designed for individuals: Part Two*. Heinemann.

Clay, M. M. (2013). An observation survey of early literacy achievement (3rd ed.). Heinemann.

Colenbrander, D., von Hagen, A., Kohnen, S., Wegener, S., Ko, K., Beyersmann, E., & Castles, A. (2024). The effects of morphological instruction on literacy outcomes for children in English-speaking countries: A systematic review and meta-analysis. *Educational Psychology Review*, 36(4), 119.

Colenbrander, D., Kohnen, S., Beyersmann, E., Robidoux, S., Wegener, S., Arrow, T., Nation, K., & Castles, A. (2022). Teaching children to read irregular words: A comparison of three instructional methods. *Scientific Studies of Reading*, 26(6), 545–564.

Concannon-Gibney, T. (2018). Immersing first graders in poetry: A genre study approach. *The Reading Teacher*, 72(4), 431-443.

Cummins, J. (1991). *BICS and CALP: Clarifying the distinction*. ERIC.

Cummins, J. (1981). Empirical and theoretical underpinnings of bilingual education. *Journal of Education*, 163(1), 16-29.

DeJulio, S., Lammert, C., Hiebert, E., Avalos, A., Cagle, B., Dean, J., Good, S., & Tice, R. (2024). CATERing to readers' needs with AI: Innovation in text design and instruction. *The Reading Teacher,* 78(1), 65–73.

Dehaene, S., & Cohen, L. (2011). The unique role of the visual word form area in reading. *Trends in Cognitive Sciences*, 15(6), 254-262.

Dolch, E. W. (1936). A basic sight vocabulary. *The Elementary School Journal*, 36(6), 456–460.

Dorofeeva, S. V., Laurinavichyute, A., Reshetnikova, V., Akhutina, T. V., Tops, W., & Dragoy, O. (2020). Complex phonological tasks predict reading in 7 to 11 years of age typically developing Russian children. *Journal of Research in Reading*, 43(4), 516-535.

Downs, J.D. (2024, February 1-2). Below grade level readers in above grade level texts? Two matched sample studies [Conference Poster]. The 32nd Annual Pacific Coast Research Conference (PCRC), Coronado, California.

Downs, J.D., Martz, K., & Bowman, W. (Manuscript in Preparation). Using the read like us protocol to read long words in challenging text.

Downs, J. D., Mohr, K. A. J., & Barrett, T. S. (2020). Determining the academic and affective outcomes of dyad reading among third graders. *The Journal of Educational Research*, 113(2), 120–132.

Downs, J., Mohr, K., & Young, C. (2023). A historical narrative review of paired oral reading practices in elementary classrooms. *Journal of Research in Reading*, 46(1), 42–63.

Downs, J., & Mohr, K. A. J. (2024). A multilevel meta-analysis of Synchronous Paired Oral Reading techniques in elementary classrooms. *Literacy Research and Instruction*, 0(0), 1–28.

Duke, N. (2022). What Wordle reminds us about effective phonics and spelling instruction. *ASCD Blog*. Arlington, VA: Association for Supervision and Curriculum Development.

Duke, N. K. (2016). Project-based instruction: A great match for informational texts. *American Educator*, 40(3), 4.

Duke, N., & Carlisle, J. (2011). The development of comprehension. *Handbook of Reading Research*. 4. 199-228.

Duke, N. K., Ward, A. E., & Pearson, P. D. (2021). The science of reading comprehension instruction. *The Reading Teacher*, 74(6), 663-672.

Ehri, L. C., & Roberts, T. (2006). The roots of learning to read and write: Acquisition of letters and phonemic awareness. *Handbook of Early Literacy Research*, 2, 113-131.

Elkonin, D. B. (1963). The psychology of mastering the elements of reading. In B. Simon and J. Simon (Eds.), *Educational psychology in the U.S.S.R.* (pp. 165-179). Routledge and Kegan Paul.

Erickson, J. D. (2019). Primary students' emic views of reading intervention: A qualitative case study of motivation. *Literacy Research: Theory, Method, Practice*, 68, 86-107.

Erickson, J. D., & Wharton-McDonald, R. (2019). Fostering autonomous motivation and early literacy skills. *The Reading Teacher*, 72(4), 475-483.

Filderman, M. J., Austin, C. R., Boucher, A. N., O'Donnell, K., & Swanson, E. A. (2022). A meta-analysis of the effects of reading comprehension interventions on the reading comprehension outcomes of struggling readers in third through 12th grades. *Exceptional Children*, 88(2), 163–184.

Filipović, L., & Hawkins, J. A. (2019). The Complex Adaptive System Principles model for bilingualism: Language interactions within and across bilingual minds. *International Journal of Bilingualism*, 23(6), 1223-1248.

Fountas, I. C., & Pinnell, G. S. (2012). *Genre study: Teaching with fiction and nonfiction books*. Heinemann.

Fountas, I. C., & Pinnell, G. S. (2017). *Literacy continuum: A tool for assessment, planning, and teaching*. Heinemann.

Freed, J., Adams, C., & Lockton E. Literacy skills in primary school-aged children with pragmatic language impairment: a comparison with children with specific language impairment. *International Journal of Language and Communication Disorders*. 2011 May-Jun;46(3):334-47.

Fry, E. (1980). The new instant word list. *The Reading Teacher*, 34(3), 284–289.

Fuchs, D., Fuchs, L.S., & Clemens, N.H. (2024, Jan 31). Challenging traditional notions of intervention in reading and mathematics [Conference panel session]. Pacific Coast Research Conference, Coronado, CA.

García, O. & Kleifgen, J. A. (2018). *Educating emergent bilinguals: Policies, programs, and practices for English learners*. Teachers College Press.

Graham, S., & Hebert, M. (2011). Writing to read: A meta-analysis of the impact of writing and writing instruction on reading. *Harvard Educational Review*, 81(4), 710-744.

Gamble, N. S., & Yates, S. (2008). *Exploring children's literature*. Sage Publications.

Gibney, T. (2012). Teaching memoir in the elementary school classroom. *The Reading Teacher*, 66(3), 243-253.

Goodrich, J. M. & Lonigan, C. J. (2017). Language-independent and language-specific aspects of early literacy: An evaluation of the common underlying proficiency model. *Journal of Educational Psychology*, 109(6),782-793.

Green, C., Keogh, K., & Prout, J. (2024). The CPB Sight Words: A new research-based high-frequency wordlist for early reading instruction. *The Reading Teacher*, 78(1), 56–64.

Groen, M., Guthrie-Veenendaal, N., & Verhoeven, L (2019). The role of prosody in reading comprehension: evidence from poor comprehenders. *Journal of Research in Reading*, 42, 37-57.

Grosjean, F. (2013). *The psycholinguistics of bilingualism.* Blackwell Publishing.

Guthrie, J. T., & Humenick, N. M. (2004). Motivating students to read: Evidence for classroom practices that increase motivation and achievement. In P. McCardle & V. Chabra (Eds.), *The voice of evidence in reading research* (pp. 329–354). Paul H. Brookes.

Hasbrouck, J. & Glaser, D. A. (2019). Reading fluency: Understand. Assess. Teach. New Rochelle, NY: PD Essentials/Benchmark Education.

Hasbrouck, J. & Tindal, G. (2017). An update to compiled ORF norms (Technical Report No. 1702). *Behavioral Research and Teaching*, University of Oregon.

Hayes, D. P., & Ahrens, M. G. (1988). Vocabulary simplification for children: A special case of 'motherese'? *Journal of Child Language*, 15(2), 395–410.

Heggie, L., & Wade-Woolley, L. (2017). Reading longer words: Insights Into multisyllabic word reading. *Perspectives of the ASHA Special Interest Groups*, 2(1), 86–94.

Hiebert, E. H. (2022). When students perform at the Below Basic level on the NAEP: What does it mean and what can educators do? *The Reading Teacher*, 75(5), 631–639.

Hiebert, E. H., Toyama, Y., & Irey, R. (2020). Features of known and unknown words for first grades of different proficiency levels in winter and spring. *Education Sciences*, 10(12), Article 12.

Horowitz, S. H., Rawe, J., & Whittaker, M. C. (2017). The state of learning disabilities: Understanding the 1 in 5. New York: National Center for Learning Disabilities.

Hoover, W. A., & Gough, P. B. (1990). The simple view of reading. Reading and Writing: *An Interdisciplinary Journal,* 2(2), 127–160.

Hulme, C., Bowyer-Crane, C., Carroll, J. M., Duff, F. J., & Snowling, M. J. (2012). The causal role of phonemic awareness and letter-sound knowledge in learning to read: Combining intervention studies with mediation analysis. *Psychological Science*, 23(6), 572-577.

Hulme, C., Hatcher, P. J., Nation, K., Brown, A., Adams, J., & Stuart, G. (2002). Phoneme awareness is a better predictor of early reading skill than onset-rime awareness. *Journal of Experimental Child Psychology*, 82, 2-28.

International Literacy Association. (2018). Literacy glossary.

Invernizzi, M., & Buckrop, J. (2018). Reconceptualizing alphabet learning and instruction. In C. M. Cassano & S. M. Dougherty (Eds.), *Pivotal research in early literacy: Foundational studies and current practices* (85-110). Guilford Press.

Ives, S. T., Wells, M., & Parsons, S. A. (2021). Autonomy-supportive classrooms. In S. A. Parsons, & M. Vaughn (Eds.), *Principles of effective literacy instruction*, K-5 (pp. 225-234). Guilford.

Joseph, J. E., & Newmeyer, F. J. (2012). 'All languages are equally complex': The rise and fall of a consensus. *Historiographia Linguistica*, 39(2-3), 341-368.

Justice, L., Kaderavek, J., Fan, X., Sofka, A., & Hunt, A. (2009). Accelerating preschoolers' early literacy development through classroom-based teacher–child storybook reading and explicit print referencing. *Language, Speech, and Hearing Services in Schools*, 40, 67–85.

Justice, L. M., Pence, K., Bowles, R. B., & Wiggins, A. (2006). An investigation of four hypotheses concerning the order by which 4-year-old children learn the alphabet letters. *Early Childhood Research Quarterly*, 21(3), 374–389.

Kaminski, R. A., & Cummings, K. D. (2007). Assessment for learning: Using general outcomes measures. *Threshold*, 26-28.

Kearns, D. M., & Hiebert, E. H. (2022). The word complexity of primary-level texts: Differences between first and third grade in widely used curricula. *Reading Research Quarterly*, 57(1), 255–285.

Kearns, D. M., Lyon, D. P., & Kelley, S. L. (2022). Structured literacy interventions for reading long words. In L. Spear-Swerling (Ed.), *Structured literacy interventions: Teaching students with reading difficulties, grades K-6* (pp. 43–64). Guilford.

Kearns, D. M., & Whaley, V. M. (2019). Helping students with dyslexia read long words: Using syllables and morphemes. *TEACHING Exceptional Children*, 51(3), 212–225.

Kilpatrick, D. A (2020). How the phonology of speech is foundational for instant word recognition. *Perspectives on Language and Literacy*, 46(3), 11-15.

Kjeldsen, A., Kärnä, A., Niemi, P., Olofsson, Å., & Witting, K. (2014). Gains from training in phonological awareness in kindergarten predict reading comprehension in grade 9. *Scientific Studies of Reading*, 18(6), 452-467.

Kroll, J.F., & Bialystok, E. Understanding the Consequences of Bilingualism for Language Processing and Cognition. *Journal of Cognitive Psychology*, 25(5).

LaBerge, D., & Samuels, S. J. (1974). Toward a theory of automatic information processing in reading. *Cognitive Psychology*, 6(2), 293–323.

Lambert, Susan. (2021). A conversation on growing up with dyslexia with 10th grader Hadyn Fleming. *The science of reading* [audio podcast], 4(12).

Landi, N., and Ryherd, K. (2017). Understanding specific reading comprehension deficit: A review. *Language and Linguistics Compass*, 11(2).

Liberman, I. Y., Shankweiler, D., Fisher, F. W., & Carter, B (1974). Explicit syllable and phoneme segmentation in the young child. *Journal of Exceptional Psychology*, 95(3), 482-494.

Loftus, M., & Sappington, L. (2024). *The literacy 50—A Q & A handbook for teachers: Real-world answers to questions about reading that keep you up at night*. Scholastic.

Lundberg, I., Frost, J., & Peterson, O. (1988). Effects of an extensive program for stimulating phonological awareness in preschool children. *Reading Research Quarterly*, 23(3), 263-284.

McCandliss, B., Beck, I., Sandak, R., & Perfetti, C. (2003). Focusing attention on decoding for children with poor reading skills: Design and preliminary tests of the word building intervention. *Scientific Studies in Reading*, 7, 75-104.

Meaningful Speech. (2023). Hyperlexia and gestalt language processing.

Melby-Lervåg, M., Lyster, S. A. H., & Hulme, C. (2012). Phonological skills and their role in learning to read: a meta-analytic review. *Psychological bulletin*, 138(2), 322-352.

Mesmer, H. A. (2024). Big words for young readers: *Teaching kids in grades K to 5 to decode—and understand—words with multiple syllables and morphemes*. Scholastic.

Miller, S. D. & Meece, J. L. (1999). Third-graders' motivational preferences for reading and writing tasks. *Elementary School Journal*, 100, 19-35.

Mo, Y., Kopke, R. A., Hawkins, L. K., Troia, G. A., & Olinghouse, N. G. (2014). The neglected "R" in a time of Common Core. *The Reading Teacher*, 67(6), 445-453.

Morgan P. L., & Fuchs, D. (2007). Is there a bidirectional relationship between children's reading skills and reading motivation? *Exceptional Children*, 73(2), 165–183.

Morrison, J.D. (2020). Dually critical: Blending Liberal-Humanist critical reading with Freirean critical literacy. *Talking Points*. 32(1), 10-19.

Murphy, P. K., Wilkinson, I. A. G., Soter, A. O., Hennessey, M. N., & Alexander, J. F. (2009). Examining the effects of classroom discussion on students' comprehension of text: A meta-analysis. *Journal of Educational Psychology*, 101(3), 740-764.

National Center for Education Statistics, National Assessment of Educational Progress. (2022). *NAEP Report Card – Reading*. US Department of Education, Institute of Education Sciences.

Orkin, M., Vanacore, K., Rhinehart, L., Gotlieb, R., & Wolf, M. (2022). The more you know: How teaching multiple aspects of word knowledge builds fluency skills. *Reading League Journal*, 3, 4-12.

Ortlieb, E. (2014). Attraction theory: Revisiting how we learn. *The Journal of Curriculum Theorising*, 30(2), 71-87.

Ostrolenk, A., Forgeot d'Arc, B., Jelenic, P. S., Fabienne, S., & Mottron, L. (2017). Hyperlexia: Systematic review, neurocognitive modelling, and outcome. *Neuroscience & Biobehavioral Reviews*, 79, 134-149.

Ozernov-Palchik, O., Norton, E. S., Sideridis, G., Beach, S. D., Wolf, M., Gabrieli, J. D.E, & Gaab, N. (2017). Longitudinal stability of pre-reading skill profiles of kindergarten children: implications for early screening and theories of reading. *Developmental Science*, 20(5), e12471–n/a.

Paige, D. D., & Rupley, W. (2024). Phonemic awareness: What skills matter and is automaticity important? (Manuscript in preparation). Department of Curriculum and Instruction, Northern Illinois University.

Parsons, S. A., & Erickson, J. D. (2024). Where is motivation in the science of reading? *Phi Delta Kappan*, 105(5), 32-36.

Paul, R. & Elder, L. (2005). Critical thinking...and the art of substantive writing, part 1. *Journal of Developmental Education*, 29(1), 40-41.

Pennington, B.F., & Olson, R. K. (2005). *Genetics of dyslexia*. The Guilford Press.

Piasta, S. B., Justice, L. M., McGinty, A. S., & Kaderavek, J. N. (2012). Increasing Young Children's Contact with Print During Shared Reading: Longitudinal Effects on Literacy Achievement. *Child Development*, 83(3), 810–820.

Puranik, C.S., Petscher, Y., Al Otaiba, S., Catts, H.W., & Lonigan, C. J. (2008). Development of oral reading fluency in children with speech or language impairments: a growth curve analysis. *Journal of Learning Disabilities*. 41(6):545-60.

Reading Rockets. Helping your child: guidance for families.

Report of the National Reading Panel: Teaching children to read. (2000). National Institute of Child Health and Human Development (NICHD) and U.S. Department of Education.

Reschly, A. L. (2009). Reading and school completion: Critical connections and Matthew Effects. *Reading & Writing Quarterly*, 26(1), 67-90.

Reutzel, D. R. (2015). Early literacy research: Findings primary grade teachers will want to know. *The Reading Teacher*, 69(1), 14-24.

Rumelhart, D.E, & McClelland, J.L. (Eds.). (1986). *Parallel distributed processing: Explorations in the microstructure of cognition, Foundations Volume 1*. Cambridge, MIT Press.

Ryan, R. M., & Deci, E. L. (2017). *Self-determination theory: Basic psychological needs in motivation, development, and wellness*. Guilford.

Savage, R. & Carless, S. (2005). Phoneme manipulation not onset-rime manipulation ability is a unique predictor of early reading. *Journal of Child Psychology and Psychiatry*, 46(12), 1297-1308.

Schiefele, U., Schaffner, E., Möller, J., & Wigfield, A. (2012). Dimensions of reading motivation and their relation to reading behavior and competence. *Reading Research Quarterly*, 47(4), 427–463.

Seravallo, J. (2015). *The reading strategies book: Your everything guide to developing skilled readers*. Heinemann.

Share, D. L. (1995). Phonological recoding and self-teaching: Sine qua non of reading acquisition. *Cognition*, 55, 151-218.

Share, D. L. (1999). Phonological recoding and orthographic learning: A direct test of the self-teaching hypothesis. *Journal of Experimental Child Psychology*, 72, 95–129.

Shea, R.H., Scanlon, L., & Aufses, R.D. (2013). *The language of composition: Reading, writing, rhetoric* (2nd ed.). Bedford/St. Martin's.

Soto, E.F., Irwin, L.N., Chan, E.S.M., Spiegel, J.A., & Kofler, M.J. Executive functions and writing skills in children with and without ADHD. Neuropsychology.

Stahl, K. A. D. (2014). New insights about letter learning. *The Reading Teacher*, 68(4), 261-265.

Stahl, S. A., & Kuhn, M. R. (2002). Making it sound like language: Developing fluency. *The Reading Teacher*, 55(6), 582-584.

Stouffer, J. (2023). Write-It-Out: A teaching response to foster complete word analysis. *The Reading Teacher*, 77(3), 414-417.

Strong, J. Z., Tortorelli, L. S., & Anderson, B. E. (2024). Read STOP Write: Teaching foundational skills in a multicomponent informational reading and writing intervention. *Journal of Adolescent & Adult Literacy*, 68(4): 339-352.

Stutz, F., Schaffner, E., & Schiefele, U. (2016). Relations among reading motivation, reading amount, and reading comprehension in the early elementary grades. *Learning and Individual Differences*, 45, 101-113.

Torgesen, J., Alexander, A., Wagner, R., Rashotte, C., Voeller, K., & Conway, T. (2001). Intensive remedial instruction for children with severe reading disabilities: Immediate and long-term outcomes from two instructional approaches. *Journal of Learning Disabilities*, 34, 33-58.

Tortorelli, L. S., Strong, J. Z., & Anderson, B. E. (2024). Multisyllabic decoding achievement and relation to vocabulary at the end of elementary school. *Journal of Experimental Child Psychology*, 246, 106018.

Toste, J. R., Capin, P., Williams, K. J., Cho, E., & Vaughn, S. (2019). Replication of an experimental study investigating the efficacy of a multisyllabic word reading intervention with and without motivational beliefs training for struggling readers. *Journal of Learning Disabilities*, 52(1), 45–58.

Toste, J. R., Didion, L., Peng, P., Filderman, M. J., & McClelland, A. M. (2020). A meta-analytic review of the relations between motivation and reading achievement for K–12 students. *Review of Educational Research*, 90(3), 420-456.

Tracht, D. (2022). Reading comprehension and executive function. *Attention Magazine*.

Traga Philippakos, Z. A., Quinn, M. F., & Rocconi, L. M. (2024). Developing multisyllabic decoding and encoding skills with upper elementary learners: Reporting two cycles of design-based research. *Reading & Writing Quarterly*, 0(0), 1–25.

Treffert, D.A. (2011). Hyperlexia III: Separating 'autistic-like' behaviors from autistic disorder; assessing children who read early or speak late. WMJ, 110(6): 281-6.

Treiman, R., & Broderick, V. (1998). What's in a name: Children's knowledge about the letters in their own names. *Journal of Experimental Child Psychology*, 70, 97-116.

Treiman, R., Hulslander, J., Olson, R. K., Willcutt, E. G., Byrne, B., & Kessler, B. (2019). The unique role of early spelling in the prediction of later literacy performance. *Scientific Studies of Reading*, 23(5), 437–444.

Turner, J. (1995). The influence of classroom contexts on young children's motivation for literacy. *Reading Research Quarterly*, 30(3), 410–441.

US Department of Education, Institute of Education Sciences, National Center for Education Statistics, National Assessment of Educational Progress (NAEP), various years, 1971–2023 Long-Term Trend Reading and Mathematics Assessments.

Vaughn, S., Gersten, R., Dimino, J., Taylor, M. J., Newman-Gonchar, R., Krowka, S., Kieffer, M. J., McKeown, M., Reed, D., Sanchez, M., St. Martin, K., Wexler, J., Morgan, S., Yañez, A., & Jayanthi, M. (2022). Providing reading interventions for students in grades 4–9 (WWC 2022007). Washington, DC: National Center for Education Evaluation and Regional Assistance (NCEE), Institute of Education Sciences, U.S. Department of Education.

Vygotsky, L. S. (1978). *Mind in society: The development of higher psychological processes*. Harvard University Press.

Weber, R.-M. (2018). Listening for schwa in academic vocabulary. *Reading Psychology*, 39(5), 468–491.

White, S., Sabatini, J., Park, B. J., Chen, J., Bernstein, J., and Li, M. (2021). *The 2018 NAEP Oral Reading Fluency Study* (NCES 2021-025). U.S. Department of Education. Washington, DC: Institute of Education Sciences, National Center for Education Statistics.

Wolf, M., & Bowers, P. G. (1999). The double-deficit hypothesis for the developmental dyslexias. *Journal of Educational Psychology*, 91(3), 415–438.

Wolf, M., & Katzir-Cohen, T. (2001). Reading fluency and its intervention. *Scientific Studies of Reading*, 5(3), 211–239.

Wyse, D., & Hacking, C. (2024). *The balancing act: An evidence-based approach to teaching phonics, reading and writing*. Taylor & Francis.

Young, C., Pearce, D., Gomez, J., Christensen, R., Pletcher, B., & Fleming, K. (2018). Read Two Impress and the Neurological Impress Method: Effects on elementary students' reading fluency, comprehension, and attitude. *The Journal of Educational Research*, 111(6), 657–665.

Young, C., Lagrone, S., & McCauley, J. (2020). Read like me: An intervention for struggling readers. *Education Sciences*, 10(3), 57.

Zutell, J., & Rasinski, T. V. (1991). Training teachers to attend to their students' oral reading fluency. *Theory Into Practice*, 30, 211-217.

About the authors

Jessica Page Bergeron, PhD, studied education and English before getting her PhD in special education from Georgia State University. With 15+ years in leadership, she is currently the Director of Outreach Services for Georgia's Office of State Schools. Passionate about literacy and early learning, she's also a dedicated single mum of two.

Wiley Blevins has a Doctorate in Education. He studied at the Harvard Graduate School of Education and Bowling Green State University. He is an author, educational consultant and researcher. Wiley has written over 17 books for teachers, as well as over 100 children's books. He is Senior Vice President and Associate Publisher at Reycraft Books.

Dr. Alta Joy Broughton is Assistant Professor of Special Education and Dyslexia Program Coordinator in the Inclusive Education Department at Kennesaw State University. Her multidisciplinary work bridges teacher education, bilingual/English Learner education, and special education.

Patricia Bryant is an experienced educator and instructional designer with a master's degree in Learning Design from Arizona State University. With over a decade of teaching and curriculum development experience, she specialises in creating engaging, interactive learning experiences for K–8 pupils and adult learners.

Dr. Ashley Carrigan, PhD, BCBA, IBA, is the Director of Training & Development at Achievements ABA Therapy, LLC, and part-time faculty at Kennesaw State University. She specialises in ACT, verbal behaviour and behaviour analytic strategies, with research on ACT-based interventions and fluency development. She holds a doctorate in Behaviour Analysis.

Keshiea Chandler is an educator with over 12 years of experience spanning classroom teaching, instructional leadership and content development. Her expertise lies in developing state-standard-aligned curricula, coaching educators, and implementing data-driven instructional strategies that enhance pupil success. She is currently pursuing her doctorate in Educational Leadership and Administration at Walden University.

L. Crosby Guard is a writer and veteran educator based in Atlanta, GA. She has taught pupils at various learning stages, from prekindergarten to post-secondary. When she is not teaching, she is reading, writing and busy keeping all of her "plates spinning".

Alison Divino Driscoll is a curriculum designer with extensive experience in developing engaging, standards-aligned educational content. She has worked across multiple subject areas, specialising in literacy, early learning, beauty, health and wellness. She holds a graduate certification in Learning Design and Technology from the Harvard Extension School.

Jake Downs is an Assistant Professor of Reading Education at Utah State University in the School of Teacher Education and Leadership. He also hosts and produces the Teaching Literacy Podcast, where he interviews reading experts to translate research into practical classroom strategies.

Lori Fromowitz is a speech language pathologist (SLP) and writer based in California. Her areas of focus include language, literacy and executive function. Lori has written several published nonfiction books for young readers and has extensive experience writing and editing literacy curriculum content.

Sarah Gannon is a former third grade teacher, reading specialist, literacy coach and Orton Gillingham practitioner. In her current role as Co-Director of Crafting Minds, Sarah translates educational research into practical strategies and curriculum resources for teachers. She resides outside of Boston with her husband and three children.

Jan Hasbrouck, PhD, is an award-winning researcher, educational consultant and author who works with schools and agencies in the US and internationally. Dr. Hasbrouck worked as a reading specialist and literacy coach for 15 years and later became a professor. Her research in reading fluency, academic assessment, interventions and instructional coaching has been widely published.

Dr. Zachary Johnson is an assistant professor of Special Education in the Inclusive Education Department at Kennesaw State University. His areas of research include both academic and behavioural strategies for pupils with high-incidence disabilities, utilising computer-based instruction and blended learning to improve their overall academic performance and engagement.

Lindsay Kemeny, MS, is an elementary school teacher, speaker, author and podcast co-host with a passion for literacy and research. After her son was diagnosed with dyslexia and depression, she began her deep dive into effective literacy instruction for all children. She is the author of the books *7 Mighty Moves* and *Rock Your Literacy Block*. She loves being in the classroom every day, teaching kids to read and write.

Melissa Loftus is a former middle school ELA teacher and district coach. She holds a BA in Education and English as well as an MEd with Reading Specialist certification and is National Board-certified.

Laura F. Main, EdD, has worked in the education field for over 30 years. She served as a founding administrator and Chief Academic Officer of Booker T. Washington Academy and Elevate Charter Schools. In this role, she wrote, developed and supported the implementation of all curricula, assessments and professional learning, including the transition to the Science of Reading.

Megan Meade has ten years of experience in preschool and kindergarten classrooms and understands what it takes for teachers to build strong readers. Now, as an instructional designer, she's sharing her expertise, equipping teachers nationwide with the science-backed tools to build confident readers.

Georgette Morgan is a Clinical Assistant Professor in the Department of Communication Sciences and Special Education at the University of Georgia. Previously, Dr. Morgan was a classroom teacher, parent educator and clinical supervisor. Her research focuses on improving the educational outcomes of individuals with developmental disabilities and autism, the strategic science of teaching, and teacher training and supervision.

Dr. Jennifer D. Morrison is an Associate Professor at Sam Houston State University. She is a National Board-certified teacher (AYA/ELA). Her experiences include being a middle and high school English teacher, gifted education resource teacher and instructional coach. She has been published in *English Journal*, *Talking Points*, *Journal of Adolescent and Adult Literacy*, *Reading Research Quarterly* and *Educational Leadership*. Dr. Morrison has won multiple awards, including the Paul and Kate Farmer English Journal Award for Writing Excellence.

Vidya Munandar is an Assistant Professor of Special Education at Kennesaw State University. She has published peer-reviewed articles on disability, autism, transition and career development. She went to college in Indonesia and earned her master's and doctoral degrees at the University of Kansas. She is from Jakarta, Indonesia, and currently lives in Atlanta, Georgia.

Evan Ortlieb is the Dean of the College of Education and Human Sciences at South Dakota State University. He is an internationally recognised leader in the field of literacy education with previous work experience in Singapore, Australia, and New York. He has published over 150 books including a series entitled *Literacy, Research, Practice and Evaluation*.

Alexandria Osburn has enjoyed her career as a special educator, reading specialist, literacy coach and Wilson Dyslexia Practitioner.

She is passionate about translating research to practise and creating educator friendly structured literacy resources. Alex lives on Lake Winnipesaukee with her loving husband.

David D. Paige is Professor of Literacy at Northern Illinois University in DeKalb, Illinois. Dr. Paige researches phonemic awareness and other processes involved in foundational skills. He also directs the Jerry L. Johns Literacy Clinic, which serves children struggling with reading.

Seth A. Parsons, PhD, is a professor in the Sturtevant Center for Literacy at George Mason University. He teaches in the Elementary Education and Literacy programmes. His books include *Accelerating Learning Recovery for All Students: Core Principles for Getting Literacy Growth Back on Track* and *Principles of Effective Literacy Instruction, K-5*.

Bethanie Pletcher is Professor of Reading Education in the Curriculum, Instruction, and Learning Sciences Department at Texas A&M University – Corpus Christi. Her research interests include literacy coaching, the design and implementation of reading clinics and supporting emergent readers who experience reading difficulties. Dr. Pletcher has published over 50 articles and book chapters and is an editor for *Literacy Research and Instruction*.

Timothy Rasinski, PhD, is professor emeritus of literacy education at Kent State University, where he was director of its award-winning reading clinic. He held the Rebecca Tolle and Burton W. Gorman Endowed Chair in Educational Leadership and was a Presidential Scholar at KSU. Tim has written over 250 articles and has authored, co-authored or edited more than 50 books or curriculum programmes on reading education. He is the author of the best-selling books on reading fluency *The Fluent Reader* and *The Megabook of Fluency*.

Tami Reis-Frankfort began teaching in a mainstream classroom in London, UK. She trained in Specific Learning Difficulties and taught struggling readers at a dyslexia center. Together with her colleagues Wendy Tweedie and Clair Wilson, she founded Phonic Books, a publishing company dedicated to creating decodable reading books to help all children learn to read.

Alexis Quinn Robinson specialises in all things education, from teaching kids to consulting with adults. As a lover of literacy instruction and a fanatic of children's literature, her passion lies in bridging the gap from Science of Reading research into effective classroom practice.

Denise Ross is a researcher in special education and applied behaviour analysis, specialising in language and literacy instruction for children with and without disabilities. She is co-editor of *When Text Speaks: Learning to Read & Reading to Learn* and co-author of *Verbal Behavior Analysis: Inducing and Expanding New Verbal Capabilities in Children with Language Delays*.

Lori Sappington is a former elementary and high school ELA teacher and district coach. She holds a BA in Elementary Education and English, an MEd with Reading Specialist certification, and an Advanced Leadership Certificate from Towson University.

Morgan Sott is a freelance educational writer from the United States. She has expertise in Multi-Tiered Systems of Support and Science of Reading content.

Elizabeth K. Waller is an adjunct field experience/seminar instructor and clinical experience coach working in the Graduate School of Education at The State University of New York at Buffalo (UB). She spent 34 years in the Buffalo Public Schools as an elementary classroom teacher, Title 1 Reading teacher, reading specialist assigned to central office, assistant principal and was Supervisor of Title 1 Reading when she retired from the district.

Kareem Weaver is the cofounder and executive director of FULCRUM, a nonprofit dedicated to fighting for children's civil right to read. He is an award-winning educator with extensive experience leading schools and systems in district, juvenile justice and managed-care settings. His advocacy is featured in the 2023 documentary *The Right to Read*.

Trina Gould Williams has over two decades of experience in education. She's honed her ability to communicate effectively and inspire curiosity. As a doctoral candidate, she constantly explores new ideas and pushes the boundaries of knowledge. When she's not writing, you might see her at her beloved alma mater, Spelman College, or listening to any true crime podcast.

Dr. Chase Young is a renowned expert in literacy education, known for his research in reading fluency, literacy interventions and effective teaching practices. He has received numerous prestigious awards, including the A.B. Herr Award, the Diane Lapp & James Flood Professional Collaborator Award, and the Jack Cassidy Award for Scholarly Contributions. With a passion for empowering educators and pupils alike, Dr. Young has authored many publications that blend research with practical classroom applications. Known for his engaging style and sense of humour, he continues to be a sought-after speaker and leader in the field of literacy education.

About the illustrator

Elen Winata is an illustrator based in Singapore. Her works span different media such as illustration, design, digital media, and advertising.

Over the years, she has provided illustrations for brands such as Adobe, Google, The Times of London, Clinique, Net-a-Porter, and Shake Shack. Her works are known for their clean lines and vibrant colours, held together by simple but thought-provoking ideas. A mix between graphic design and art, her style brings together functionality and aesthetics.

When she's not pushing pixels, you can find her drinking tea, doodling quotes, or stalking the neighbourhood cat.

Produced for DK by
Editorial Westchester Publishing Services
Design and Jacket Louise Brigenshaw
Illustrator Elen Winata

Project Editor Amanda Eisenthal
Managing Editor Carine Tracanelli
Managing Art Editor Sarah Corcoran
Pre-Production Coordinator Shanker Prasad
Pre-Production Designer Rohit Singh
Production Controller Isabell Schart
Publisher Sarah Forbes
Managing Director, Learning Hilary Fine

First American Edition, 2026
Published in Great Britain by Dorling Kindersley Limited
20 Vauxhall Bridge Road, London SW1V 2SA

Copyright © 2026 Dorling Kindersley Limited
A Penguin Random House Company
10 9 8 7 6 5 4 3 2 1
001–348717–Jan/2026

All rights reserved.
No part of this publication may be reproduced, stored in or introduced into a retrieval system, or transmitted, in any form, or by any means (electronic, mechanical, photocopying, recording, or otherwise), without the prior written permission of the copyright owner.
DK values and supports copyright. Thank you for respecting intellectual property laws by not reproducing, scanning or distributing any part of this publication by any means without permission. By purchasing an authorised edition, you are supporting writers and artists and enabling DK to continue to publish books that inform and inspire readers. No part of this publication may be used or reproduced in any manner for the purpose of training artificial intelligence technologies or systems. In accordance with Article 4(3) of the DSM Directive 2019/790, DK expressly reserves this work from the text and data mining exception.

A CIP catalogue record for this book is available from the British Library.
ISBN 978-0-2417-3284-7

Printed and bound in China

www.dk.com

This book was made with Forest Stewardship Council™ certified paper – one small step in DK's commitment to a sustainable future.
Learn more at www.dk.com/uk/information/sustainability